RISE FROM WITHIN

On behalf of the writers, authors, and 300 South Media Group, I'd like to thank you for your interest in Rise From Within, for reading the stories shared on these pages, and for giving a voice to the words.

Jay Long

For more information on each contributing author, please refer to the ABOUT THE AUTHORS section at the end of the book.

We also invite you to follow Rise From Within on Facebook, where the authors and more of their writing will be featured.

FACEBOOK.COM/WERISEFROMWITHIN

RISE FROM WITHIN

an anthology of poetry, prose, essays, & short stories

300 SOUTH MEDIA GROUP

NEW YORK

This book is presented as a collection.

ISBN-13: 978-0-9970356-3-6

First Printing December 2020

Cover & Interior Design by 300 South Media Group

300SMG.com

Printed in the United States of America

DEDICATION

We all find ourselves in a darkened room from time to time. For those who fight the demons daily, may the sun continue to shine until you can finally find the light.

Jay Long

TABLE OF CONTENTS

PREFACE

2020 has been like nothing any of us have experienced as a whole. On a personal level, the downside of good started at the very end of December 2019 and continued into the new year, and ultimately bled into the last 9 months of the COVID-19 crisis.

Aside from my own tragedies, I was witness to dark times that many of my close friends were experiencing. Again, most of it hitting during a worldwide pandemic.

My thoughts often wandered to one glaring question--'How do we come back from all of this?" At the time, I didn't have the answer, but one thing that was certain, through it all, life goes on. Looking back that thought was the seed that was planted leading to this anthology being born.

As the days passed it seemed the more we wanted things to go back to normal, they instead grew further away from the center. But what I noticed was we did come together--we tried our best to be empathetic to others and their situations. We were all doing our best to keep our eyes on the shoreline even during days we thought we'd surely drown.

I started seeing families come together--closer than they were. I saw business owners adapting to the new rules and making ends meet the best they could. And I saw a friend who had left a very toxic and violent relationship find their voice once again.

It was then the epiphany came--we can't rely on a manufactured system which we have no control of. The only way back is to find strength in ourselves. In all the chaos we must find peace and rise from within.

Jay Long
300 South Media Group

INTRODUCTION

When submissions for Rise From Within began, I had no idea what to expect. There were no restrictions on the type of pieces to be considered for inclusion. What followed was amazing.

What started off as an idea has become a work of art.

80 writers from 5 continents contributed to this masterpiece. Their words were not censored, the text was left the way they wrote it--the way it was intended—100% raw and real.

Rise From Within is a collection of poems, essays, prose, creative non-fiction, and fictional short stories. Within these pages, writers share pieces of surviving life and overcoming its challenges.

It is important to note, some of the stories within contain instances of domestic violence, early abuse, thoughts of suicide, rape, and other struggles that may go unseen by most but are all too real for those who have experienced it.

I couldn't be more proud of all those who made this book possible. Vulnerability is certainly the fuel for creativity. I am humbled to share with you these words--these stories--these truths.

Jay Long

300 South Media Group

C.N. GREER

GRAVEYARD OF BROKEN DREAMS

See her from the inside out
and you'd think she's been through war.
Her soul's been bruised and tattered.
Her sense of self is torn.
There are bullet holes in her armor
stab wounds through her chest.
Her hands hold shattered pieces.
Broken ribs protect the rest.
Her arms are black and mottled
from the blows that they call love.
She's felt the blade so many times
her tears have dried in blood.
Her scars are her companions
her ghosts the penance that she reaps.
Her eyes are sad and haunted
from the secrets that she keeps.
Her heart is marred by stitches
that tear each time it beats
as she wanders through the graveyard
of second chances and broken dreams.

C.N. Greer

MY ADDICTION

I've never been a drug addict. I'm not an alcoholic, a gambler. I'm not a victim of domestic violence—physically, anyway. I've never had to cover a bruise with makeup or use glasses to hide my eyes. I wasn't beaten as a kid and I don't come from a broken home. That doesn't mean that I don't bleed. That my soul isn't shredded into tangled threads. That my nails aren't a bloody mess from clawing my way out of my own version of Hell. It's not a competition. The horrors of my past may not be logged in court files, but my trials are just as real, and my struggle has almost killed me.

You see, I'm addicted to my pain. To the sweet agony of despair, demanding to be felt. The depression is dark and deep, the memories like drugs in my system, taking me on a high I have no desire to explain. It let me escape the demands of my own reality as if my days were spent on a stage. But my nights were filled with blood and tears, restless hours, and endless stitches as I sewed my pieces back into something resembling a human being.

The trust I let someone betray, the acts I agreed to endure to end the merciless attacks on my psyche, haunt my dreams in the lonely hours. The demons destabilizing the emotions I already felt in the extremes, the anguish that washed over me, became a delicious torment, a high that would let me disappear beneath the waves of tragedy and torture, the feeling like razor blades against my skin.

Yet, to the world, I still looked whole. I had no bruises to show the masses, no scars, or track marks to prove my suffering was real. All I had were the endless nights and horrifying knowledge that all the pain I felt was inside my head, and the one terrorizing my heart time after time…was me. So, I told no one. For years, I suffered in silence. It's a miracle I've finally learned to breathe. Some of us aren't so lucky.

C.N. Greer

ANNE BIRKELBAW

I RAN

I just ran.

I screamed until I tasted my own blood and could smell my fear in the air. It was as if I had been taken over by a survival instinct that sent me out that door and down that dirt driveway. I knew hell was behind me and my friend's cries clung to the desperate air. She was being beaten for protecting me, and this other nightmare in human skin was chasing me. Everything went dark, and my mind went to a place reserved only for those who fall face-first into madness.

I spent the next two years in a trauma-induced fog navigating the justice system while simultaneously experiencing a complete and utter mental breakdown. The person I was had been replaced with a person I never wanted to be, and the people around me reflected the war of self-hate raging inside myself. The strong woman I once was had been replaced with a terrified little girl who trembled in the courtroom without a voice. Even though I ran to save both my friend and I's life that day, I no longer had the will to live. Seeing evil face to face had fractured something deep in my core, and just existing had become just too painful.

I only had two choices at that point. I could continue being the victim who ran for her life that day, or I could learn to walk the path of healing into a survivor. I could no longer marinate in the horror that my life had become. I fought for this life and now I needed to learn to actually live it. I kept feeling this spark of a woman trying to claw her way out. I had never seen her face before, but she just had this sense of warmth that beckoned me to stay. So, I chose to stop running the day I walked into a therapist's office, sat down in her chair, and began to heal.

The last time I faced my perpetrators I did so steady on my feet, head held high, and without fear. I saw first-hand what an unhealed life had created in them, and I refuse to become the monsters that dominated my life for way too long. As painful as the entire thing had been, I am somehow oddly grateful. Without my time in hell, I would have never faced my greatest fears and failures. I would have never learned the grace and freedom of healing. I would have never met that tiny spark of a woman who had been silently waiting inside me to become a raging fire of hope. I would have never learned to stop running.

Anne Birckelbaw

COLEEN C KIMBRO

EMBRACE YOUR PAIN

Embrace your pain and remind it of who the FUCK you are!
Allow your pain to keep you company only briefly, then kindly show
it to the door. Remind yourself, as often as needed, that you are a
stronger person now who is more secure. You now have more self-
esteem and self-confidence. You no longer crumble when pain comes
calling and knocking on your door. You are a beautiful Warrior who
has survived Hell and the Devils that tried to bring you down. You
have dusted your broken wings off and rose like a Phoenix ascending
from your pain. You've shown everyone that you are capable of not
only surviving but also overcoming any and everything! Let your
Pain be a Reminder of who the FUCK YOU ARE!

Coleen C Kimbro

OVERCOMING

We each have it in us to overcome obstacles that life and other humans throw our way. We must simply believe in ourselves enough to know that we are capable of overcoming any and everything. If we as an individual do not put forth the effort into believing in ourself, how then can we blame others for their lack of faith or their lack of belief in us?

The solution is simple, wake up each morning and look in the mirror and say "Good Morning Beautiful. Today is going to be an amazing day because I am worth it!"

Tell yourself what you need to hear; I am Smart, Funny, Unique, Talented, Charming, Loving, Encouraging, etc. And before too long, your perception of yourself will change as well as the perception others have of you. Once you have this figured out, nothing can stop you!

Your future depends on your ability to overcome and move forward. Let your past guide you, but never allow it to keep you prisoner. Use all of your strength and determination to Rise above anything that has tried to destroy you and once the storm is over, use what you know to help another struggling soul overcome and win their battle.

Coleen C Kimbro

DALENA DUCO

HEROIN ADDICTION

I started out on weed
It wasn't enough
I wanted something more
Oxycontin got the job
Soon growing weed
To sell for smack
Because Oxycontin
Soon did jack
It was in the house
They called the barn
I first pumped death
Into my arm
Mentally hooked
From that first hit
Could've died any time
I didn't give a shit
With a melting pot
Of brand new firsts
Never say never
Where this drug's concerned

The never wills
Become the norm

Pierce your skin
An addict's born

Little Miss H
So relentless
Drop kicked into
Hell on earthness
Too numb to love
Anything but the drug
React to danger
With a "meh" shrug
A bruised up body
Was normal violence
Little things caused
World War '90
Rotting teeth
Abscessed veins
Lose it all and
Nothing's gained
Homelessness
Possessions sold
Gain a rap sheet
Sleep in the cold

More never wills
Become a cert
A raging sea
Of precious hurt
Every standard
Bites the dust

No real friends left
No one to trust

You fucking hate
Who you've become
"Friends" drop dead
One by one
It wasn't until
My final fall
I realized I'd
Almost lost it all
My last overdose
Saved me that day
It was on my son's
Tenth birthday

Dalena Duco

DONNA DAWKIN

LEARNING TO SPEAK AGAIN

And then…
It was just safer.
I was gonna say easier
But yea, safer is the right word.
Safer to smile and not have a comment
Stifle the voice that never knew the right words
Smile and agree, because isn't that just what you wanted anyway?
There I was, lost, alone
And that place is so…
Not even dark.
Just bland and beige with no heart, no beat
I have tried to find my way out
And tried to open the doors
But it's safer.
I won't hurt you and you can't hurt me, anymore.
Safer
It's not even a death
It's just, eternally on hold.
What is happening now?
This barely concealed emotion
That keeps trying to find a crack
To let in the light,
and sometimes the dark...

Rise From Within

I fear that step, away from the safe
But beige no longer looks good on me.
And even if my truth
Is different than yours
Let us grow from that
Not hide from it.
And so, if I start to disagree
Or suddenly have strange opinions…
They are not new
But my voice is, and I am only
Learning to speak again.

Donna Dawkin

ROOTS

Do you ever feel like that single lone tree?
Braced against the raging current of an avalanche
Determined to hold your ground
But overwhelmed by the mass of energy sweeping past you
Just trying to gather you up and drag you along

Is there ever a time you wonder
Am I facing the wrong way?
How is it that all foundations but my own
Have let go to tumble along safe in their numbers
Unstoppable in their masses

Never give up the fight
Wind those roots deeply
Wrap them tightly around your core, your truths
And hang on. I will stand there with you
Here, hold my hand.

Donna Dawkin

CAROLINE CARTER

EGG SHELLS

My steps were never meant to be marked
by the shards of your fragile ego.

Each footfall not feathered,
but powerfully placed.

Each and every stride of mine
was meant to be heavy
with nothing but healing.

I walked away from your glass house.
I kicked the damn door down
and shattered the mirrors on my way out.

I crashed and I crumbled
as I watched it come down.

I reached my hand forward
to drag myself up,
and for the first time
I wasn't met with your razor blades against my soles.

It took me years to remove the splinters,
and even now some still remain.

But they serve to remind me
to never step foot in your glass house again.

Caroline Carter

UNBORN, BUT NEVER UNLOVED

Then he asked me how I was doing
and I spilled over,
like paint cans of red and black and grey.
It was dark and muddy and messy.
I was never good at that lie,
the one where you say that you're fine,
like your world wasn't just ripped from your gut
leaving you empty and hollow.
I know eventually,
those paint cans will stop spilling
and I'll dip my brush into blues and greens and pinks.
I'll paint myself in fields of wildflowers in full bloom,
but today I sit in hell,
grasping my brush in my trembling hands,
wishing for the strength to paint a new day,
one without you,
but with sunshine.

> *I wrote this piece for the families who suffer miscarriage,
> abortion (whether forced or regretted), the loss of a child,
> or the inability to conceive. We rise every day, but it
> never becomes easier. We've just learned to paint our
> own sunrise.*

Caroline Carter

SOL RISING

You watch the sunset,
And the pinks skies.
You find comfort in my night times.
But with every midnight
Comes a sunrise,
Where the rays gleam
And burn your eyes.
I'm not snuffed out.
I'm not held down.
I'm not silenced
When you hear no sound.
It's in this quiet
That I am found,
Like the sunrise
I'll come 'round.
I'll set fire to your morning,
Rush in with no warning,
Climb high behind noon clouds,
Only to peak out
And to scream loud.

I was not darkened.
I was not dimmed.
Watch me now,
As I rise from within.

Caroline Carter

A. SHEA

THROUGH THE DARK

With blurry eyes
and a bruised heart,
she saw herself
through the dark.
With a hint of life
and hope so thin...
she was her own miracle
in the end.

A. Shea

PHOENIX FIRE

I was never
rainbows and butterflies
born into a life
of cloudy, death grip days.
I am Phoenix fire
and silver linings...
the things that saved me.

A. Shea

DARKNESS GROWS

What the darkness grows
it does not own.
Emerge from the shadows
with a glow
so strong the angels
turn their face,
so ruthless the demons
fear your name.

A. Shea

CHARLENE ANN BENOIT

RISE

5 a.m.,
the sun rises.
She rises from her bed,
slides on her favourite slippers,
boils water to make tea,
watches the steam rise in the air.

She gets dressed in her comfy clothes,
then realizes she is freezing...
yet can't decide
which part of her is cold.
She puts another log on the fire,
and watches the smoke rise.

It's nearly noon.
She tries to remember
exactly what her mother said,
but the words of comfort aren't coming.
She looks out the window at the rising tide,
and feels a change in her current.

Tired of being tired,
a self-contained prisoner to her cottage walls.
She heads to her bedroom, raises the lid of her suitcase
packs a bag that will never see her closet again.

She drives off towards a new beginning.
Like the sun, the steam, the smoke, and the tide...

She's going to rise.

Charlene Ann Benoit

AFTER THE RAIN

He was sad, and more often than not, that sadness would manifest itself as irritability with everything in his life. He woke up every morning hating the person he saw in the mirror and felt so isolated that he constantly bounced between anger and melancholy. He never wanted to talk about what was bothering him, but I could tell by the faraway look in his eyes that something was wrong... and it never went away. It was like a dark cloud followed him, and, like with any dark cloud, I knew it was only a matter of time before it rained.

He would submerse himself so deeply into his work, that by Valentine's Day, he barely had time for me. He still tried to show me how much he loved me, but I knew something was missing. We mutually agreed, that regardless of how much we loved each other, we needed to just be friends. We took new directions in our lives, yet still kept in touch.

I will never forget when the rain came pouring down. We were talking about his family, life, school... therapist. At first, I was taken aback; I hadn't realized things had gotten to the point where he sought professional help. I told him I wished he had come to me sooner, but he cut me off and said, "I have decided that I want to be a woman." I just sat there for a moment. I was shocked. I was prepared for anything other than that. It was in that moment that my heart became overwhelmed with grief. The man that I had once loved so fiercely was no more.

I composed myself and asked if she was certain. She told me that she was confident in her decision, and deep down it was something she'd always known. I cracked a joke about not being interested in women, but no matter what, I still loved her. This wasn't about me. It was about her and what she needed to be happy. At the end of the day, she was still my friend, the keeper of many of my secrets, and the person who often knew me better than I knew myself. Though I could never comprehend feeling I was born the wrong gender, I knew how it felt not being comfortable in my own skin.

The months passed and she began to shine like the sun after the rain. She had left behind the darkness with all of the black clothing and began wearing colors that were as soft, bright, and happy, a reflection of how she now felt inside. She laid the image of who the world told her to be to rest and rose from within. She became outgoing and an active member in the LBGTQ+ community. The dark things "he" had surrounded himself with were gone.

I am proud to know her, even prouder to call her my friend. Though she still struggles with the process of transitioning, her decision and determination have turned her into one of the bravest people I know. She said, "In life, you have to face adversities, how you handle them and push forward is what shows your true character and courage." As much as I miss the man that I fell in love with, I will always carry his memory with me. I was fortunate enough to end up with a new friend who could talk about the memories I built with him. At the end of the day, when you truly love someone, you need to be supportive when they discover what makes them happy and at peace; it's the very thing we are all searching for. I am grateful to her... she let me love her twice.

Charlene Ann Benoit

DIONA RODGERS

ONE DAY

One day,
You will meet the man of your dreams.
Sweetheart,
I know how hard it is for you to wait.
You were with someone for so long.
And then,
You had to start over.
I know it's been hard.
But through all of this,
You have become a stronger, more independent woman.
A woman you can be proud of!
A woman I am proud of!
Don't allow your loneliness to settle for anything less,
For nothing but the best will do.
I want you to truly feel what it feels like for someone to love you
Through thick and thin.
Through ups and downs.
Through ins and outs.
Someone who only has eyes for you,
And who loves and respects you enough to not allow
His eyes or mind to wander.
Someone you will be able to trust with your life.
You know as well as I do
That this new life won't end up
In a happily ever after.

No,
But it will end up with a life
That you only dreamed of having, in times past.
So please,
Hang tight while you hang tough.
It will come about.
I know it will.
And I pray that it will be

One day,

Soon.

Diona Rodgers

STARTING OVER

I sit here
Drowning in sorrow
Because I don't know what to do
Or where to go.
Starting over has not been the easiest thing for me.
I wish I could say that it has,
But it hasn't.
Many times,
I still feel so lost
And so alone.
I just want to crawl in a hole and withdraw from the world for the rest
of my days.
But that simply isn't realistic.
I have children who depend on me
To keep going,
Even when things come crashing down so hard
That I just want to escape and give up forever.
I have never been a quitter.
My marriage proved that a thousand times over
Until the abuse was too much to bear,
And I had to do what was best for the children and I.
Things changed drastically
And for the better
After he left.
I don't ever want to go back.
I lost my identity when I married,
And I want it back so badly.
I can't go back to who I was before then, however.

Rise From Within

I have changed too much.
I expected things to be a little easier
Starting over,
But it hasn't.
In some ways,
It has been more difficult.
It was as if I was already a single mother
When the ex was still around.
I became the head of household
And made sure everything was taken care of,
Mainly for the sake of the children.
Everything was up to me,
As it is now.
So each day,
I wake up more resolved than ever to figure things out,
So that I can make a better life for the children still dependent upon
me.
It's not about the riches.
It's about the quality of life.
I want to live in peace and safety,
So I continue to build a home
Whose foundation is love.

Diona Rodgers

DAWN P. HARRELL

DEEP HOLLOWS

There can be oceans of hurts inside your soul.
Gullies washed open by tears you didn't even know you cried.
Some come fresh to your mind, and often, reminding you of some
perceived failure or misstep you may have made.

Mocking your resolve to get better. Wanting to drag you back down.
Some just a feeling of sadness that you can't find a reason for
throughout the day.

Some like me learn to live this way. Taking almost comfort in the
sadness.

Seems better on some days than clawing back to the way things used
to be.

I still go there. In the deep hollows of my mind.
But I'm learning that I can find a way to fill in some of the holes.
Maybe get out and walk and feel the sun warming my face. Some
days I can and it's magic.

Take care of me even if I don't feel like it. Baby steps.

Can you grab a shovel and fill in the holes of that gully with the
shame and guilt that was never really yours to bear? Bury it, building
a foundation of love for the things you forgot gave you meaning?

27

Rise From Within

Some days I can't. But now I'm okay with that. On days like today I'm feeling the tears behind my eyes and willing them not to come. As I look out on a beautiful yard covered in a dusting of colored leaves and feel grateful.

Let's get up and find some hope. Keep burying those things you weren't meant to have. There is meaning in the glimmers we see of who we were meant to be. It's beautiful and you so deserve it.

Dawn P. Harrell

THE SHATTERING

Some days I still feel like the little girl who lost her mother
and tried to pick up where her Mom left off to keep from shattering
Wish I would have known back then
how many ways there were to shatter
Maybe I'd have known sooner that it's okay;
all of the pieces don't fit quite like they did before
Everyone is not going to love the way you love
Some days the physical bruises hurt less than the ones in your mind
You got away
Then you relearn how to live
A little differently, as you had to rearrange the pieces that were left
And you feel the wind blow through the cracks and chill your resolve
To build that better life
But still, you rise
Maybe not every day but most
But it becomes alright cause you become easier on yourself
And bit by broken bit it happens
You feel good in your skin
Sometimes out of nowhere, a grin
That little girl is still there
But you are there for her now
And there's hope
In the shattering

Dawn P. Harrell

ELIZABETH

OLD SOULS

His heart beats like the next one,
except when she is near -
skipping ahead or stalling -
this, his only fear

Will she love me if she sees my scars?

He knows she'll never hurt him,
a trust he can't explain
why he can't deny the thought
for she has had her share of pain

Will she crush me if I give her my heart?

What he didn't understand
is just how gentle her hands
could protect his fragile heart
When she, herself, was scattered about
in pieces and in parts

Will she remember me long after dark?

He showed her what he couldn't say,
loved everything she held at bay
No guards were up,

no spirits were down
Within their shared silence,
a pure love was found
Two old souls, familiar from the past,
Found each other,
finally,
at last

elizabeth

AFRAID, NOT

I've been the quiet one for far too long.

I used to be afraid of my own words, my thoughts voiced for everyone. The raised eyebrows always caught my eye, but the awkward stares and speechless distance left marks. Even greater were the snickers and the "you're crazies".

I used to be afraid of the amount of emotional depth I felt, buried, and kept hidden; I mastered the art of detachment and disconnection. I was ashamed by how deeply I was affected by my surroundings, by other people...humanity across the globe.

I used to be afraid of the pain I felt. Labeled a hypochondriac as a child, empathic living is a curse and a blessing. Ridiculed and hurt for showing any emotion, I learned which mask to wear when -

except around the creatures. I was the most free around the furred and feathered.

I used to be afraid if people saw the hidden me. Only a few special people in my adult life have seen me without any of my masks. I found solace in writing, poetry mostly. It's my therapy and my raw truth; it's what my soul sings proudly, and quietly screams when I cannot, mask-free.

I am no longer afraid of me. I am a deeply emotional person, and I wouldn't want it any other way. I wouldn't want to live this life absent of any feeling, or half-feeling. There is no sorta tired in my world; I'm either conscious or exhausted. I'm ecstatic or I'm devastated. I either fiercely love you unconditionally, or I don't.

But if I do...look out, as most likely you'll never know what hit you
and I hope you can swim as my soul is deep,
and I am a raging storm.

elizabeth

CYCLES AND SEASONS

He didn't put me where I am
I followed my heart down a crooked road
Thinking I could handle the bumps, curves, and holes
I kept driving right on through all the lies
(tears streaming from my eyes)

Will you watch over me?
Through the cycles and the seasons
Carefully guiding my path,
Justify my reasons
Let me falter, let me rise
So I can be stronger
On the other side
And get there on my own

He didn't have to raise a hand
I watched his words damage more
Wanting to erase everything he ever said, ever told
I let the silence lead me back home
(solitude is the blanket for the soul)

Will you please carry me?
Through the cycles and the seasons
Carefully covering up my path,
Explain all the reasons
How I've wondered, how I've tried
Will I be stronger
On the other side

Rise From Within

And stand on my own

He didn't even give a damn
I wore his ring of broken promises
Wishing I could just polish out the hurt and blind the truth
I untwist the gold until I'm bruised
(leaving a mark of the used)

Will you come walk with me?
Through the cycles and the seasons
Carefully paving a new path,
Give me solid reasons
Help me grow, make me shine
I will be stronger
On the other side
And not stand alone
...Without you...

elizabeth

GROUND

FOR MY FATHER

That day the sun was a foe without mercy, its violent light peered into my soul as if it to mock me.

I needed the clouds to weep with me, I needed a downpour, a storm- anything to reflect what I felt, anything to appease the sorrow.

That day my mind raced, my heart crushed with rage cursed the echoes of dormant memories.

That day...I lost a piece of my history,

I lost a voice that would comfort me; I lost a generation of a heart's wealth, so I asked myself, how do you mourn a king.

These words are my mourning and my rise as I'm adorned in the memory of you.

For my father.

Ground

IZZAH ALVI

MIRROR, MIRROR

Mirror mirror on the wall
Come, let's take this fall
Together
For I don't understand why
When I am shattered
You stand tall
Not a single crack I see
Aren't you the reflection of me?
I don't know your secrets
But you know mine
I am bruised, scarred
Yet you shine
I am here again
Waiting for a sign
Is there still time?
I can hear the alarms going off
The church bells ring
Why don't you sing?
A goodbye song
But I don't see you going
Just not yet
Oh I bet
This chest of yours
Must feel heavy
In a curled up body

You're scared, locked away
You're looking for the key
And it's a sign
You want to be free
Here, have your wings
And take off
For the person in the mirror
Will never be enough

Izzah Alvi

JANDERSON

PHOENIX WITHIN

Shattered
My soul is broken
My heart in shards
The voice within
Me
Screaming
HELP ME
…but no one hears
No one cares

They don't see
The wounds
Deep within

Function
Maintain
Get through each day

Breathe
…just breathe

But I just
Wanna scream
HELP ME

Like a child
In the cold, dark night
I've lost my way
The path too steep
Laden with hazards
Footing is unsure
The way so unclear
The crumbs I thought
I'd left
Are gone
Nothing to lead
Me
Nothing to show me the way
Fear embraces me
Strangles me
Threatens to take me down
Oh my God
Will I ever again
See the light of day

Clawing my way out of
The womb of despair
Breaking through
Layer after layer
Membranes of emotion
Each "hurdle" overcome
A rebirth
Clean slate
Renewal

Rejuvenation

I am clawing my way
From the womb of despair

JAnderson

JENNIFER JENNINGS DAVES

FLY

Change is hard
Change cuts deep
Right to the core
Of my very being
But I must change
I need to change
For me
For my sanity
For my health
You were supposed to forge
Ahead in life together
But you have us spinning in circles
Never leading us anywhere
You were in charge of the reins
But you let them hang loose
Why, I do not know
But I am tired of circles
It is time for me to take control
Mirrors can lie
And I do not wish
To wait for a landslide
My life is worthy
Of having real love
I am tired of this cage
Whatever it takes

I promise you
I will break free
From this circle of nowhere
From this death grip of lovelessness
I will be free
I will walk in the sun once more
And this bird will finally
Sing songs of joy forevermore

Jennifer Jennings Daves

OUT OF THE ASHES

No more am I the young girl
Innocent and naive
The springtime of youth
Has left me behind
To dance with another
Summer blazes through
With its passionate heat
And embers become
Abundant, warming my feet
As the autumn of life approaches me
The dance may be slower
But the colors are bright and true
As I embrace the grace that I am

Becoming a soldier of the passage of time
Fighting to free myself from the chains
Created by spring's folly
And ignored by summer's heated airs
As the passage of time dwindles slower
I gaze upon the life that remains
And whisper to friend winter
That my coming will be at a slow gait
I am in no hurry
To meet my final chapters
But these smoldering ashes
Surrounding me calling
For me to rise
Like a Phoenix
Out of the ashes

Jennifer Jennings Daves

THE LAZARUS MAN

For most people, fall signifies the coming of holidays and family
gatherings. Piles of colorful leaves spring up in yards seemingly
overnight. The crisp air and shorter days give way to football games
and hot chocolate.

For others, including Lonnie, fall meant a once a year trip to a more
western state to partake in another tradition, elk hunting. He wasn't a

trophy hunter. He had saved up what he could from his carpentry job to make the trip to Colorado to obtain meat to fill his freezer for the coming year.

In the days leading up to the trip, he had planned and packed what he knew he needed. A stubborn cough and seasonal cold, however, had started to plague him. He didn't think too much of it though, as he was a pretty healthy guy and only in his thirties.

He had planned to meet his cousins at the campsite once he got there. They were, sadly, running behind and were not there when he left to go scouting that first day. Lonnie hiked a good twenty miles that day and by the time he got back to his truck, he was weary and very much out of breath. The cough was still irritating as well. He had made a camper in the bed of his truck and was quite toasty. With temperatures falling along with the snow, he decided to hunker down for the night; hoping his cousins would make it by morning. However, due to the hike and that cold, he did not feel like eating much and went on to sleep.

He woke up in the middle of the night barely able to breathe. He tried to take a few deep breaths but all he could do was weeze and take short, quick gulps of air. He thought, Lord, I must have pneumonia. So after mustering up some strength, he decided he would go down the mountain into Laramie, Wyoming to see a doctor as it was the closest town that would have one.

But first, he had to bust out of the bed of his truck. The snow that had fallen during the night and melted and refroze, sealing the door of the camper shut. Once in the cab, Lonnie cranked the truck and wound his way down the mountain.

His body, however, was starting to rebel and wanted to shut down. He passed out and wrecked several times on his way to Laramie. The last time, his truck ended up straddling the head of the river. It was barely a creek, but his truck went from one side to the other. It was again snowing so bad that it was nearly whiteout conditions. In the distance, Lonnie saw a light and heard a dog barking. As he slowly walked towards the light, he heard a voice call out, "Can I help you?"

Lonnie couldn't believe his ears and finally, he was able to see a barn with a bunkhouse attached. On the porch was an old cowboy in his longjohns, who looked up and again asked, "Can I help you?"

Lonnie explained that he was sick and needed to get to a doctor and that he had wrecked his truck, which was now straddling the head of the Laramie River. The old cowboy got the tractor, a large eight tired John Deere, and pulled Lonnie's truck out of the river and back onto the road. Lonnie thanked him for his help and started back on his way to Laramie. After searching for a doctor, he ended up at the ER in Laramie's hospital.

At first, Lonnie thought that the doctor was just going to give him some meds for the pneumonia, which is all he really wanted. However, both his body and the doctor had other plans. He didn't just have pneumonia. A virus had attacked his heart and he was starting to go into congestive heart failure. "But I am as strong as an ox!" Lonnie declared.

Things soon became very touch and go and the doctor thought he needed more specialized care that only the doctors in Cheyenne, Wyoming could give him. A cardiology team was ready to receive him, but due to the weather, they would be transporting him by ambulance rather than by helicopter. It was slow going over those icy roads, but the ambulance finally made it. As they rushed him inside, his heart stopped beating. Frantically working the doctors and nurses set to revive him and he was hooked up to a machine that took over the duties of his heart. Once alert enough, Lonnie had to make a call home to his mom and then a call to social security to inform them that he was never going to be able to work a public job again. It took two weeks for his heart to really start working again.

He was then finally released to go home to North Carolina, his mom by his side. The doctors only gave him a ten percent chance to live for six months. He couldn't even walk the full length of the hallway in his house when he arrived home. But miracles do happen. The six months went by and in that time, his normal color came back and he could walk the hallway without getting winded. Four and a half years later, we met and got married. Now, with two kids here, we are set to celebrate our 21st wedding anniversary in November. He defied all odds and is a walking medical miracle.

Jennifer Jennings Daves

KRISTIN KORY

BEYOND THE DEPTHS OF BONES

I'm a work in progress, in a perpetual state of becoming. I unravel. It's what I do. I've shed numerous skins. I've been many women; some failed me and betrayed me, others hurt me and embarrassed me. But damn, did they teach me.

The unraveling is continuous. I don't come undone, I am undone. So fucking undone; constantly evolving and becoming. I've grown amidst the chaos, pushed through cracks in the foundation, beyond the confines of self-doubt; I've shed so many skins that I've lost count.

It's not pretty, it never is. The lessons are in the ugly parts. You find them when the blinders come off and you allow yourself to catch a glimpse of the ugliness that stirs beneath the surface. This is where the denial ends and the seeing begins. This is where you step outside yourself and peer down into your own dark depths; the abyss, the sleeping giant that awaits you—beyond the depth of bones, the darkest place I've ever known.

I was there, at the bottom and I will tell you this: Down there, you no longer need denial to soften the blow because you are ready to face your demons. Down there, nothing stands in your way. It's just you and the sound of your soul and up is the only way to go. You climb, you fight, you rise.

Rise From Within

Sometimes I've got it together, sometimes I don't. Sometimes I love myself, sometimes the jury is still out. I'm full of flaws, I'm a pro at making mistakes and I'm not sure if I'll ever get things right, but I'm here, I'm showing up, and I am trying.

Kristin Kory

LINDI BAIRD

SHADOW WITHIN

We grow up with hopes and dreams
but shatter the hearts of the ones we love so dear!
Tug of wars while challenging the cores!
They keep on asking 'why can't u just be like the rest of us!'
U look back over three decades and wonder
could I have done things differently?
People say you can forget but I firmly believe
that's a myth as the scars always remain.
Those around you just remember
the destruction you caused and will cling onto them.
They'll try and break your spirit by reminding
you of your past mistakes.
You turn your back on them all,
disappearing into a world of your own.
Isolation becomes your new best friend.
You stand tall and face it alone.
An incident happens, false accusations will lead to a dismissal.
You keep your head up high as you know the evidence against you
is weak and petty, yet the instigator wants to set an example, and
what better way to use you as the pawn for others to see and fear.
You walk away with a torn heart
and think maybe it's time for a brand new start.
Those with whom you once shared a working relationship
will distant themselves just to save their own skin.
Then the true challenge begins.

Survival is the key.
Soon you need to let go of everything you once held dear.
Things that you have accumulated over the years
everything will be ripped away.
It challenges your faith.
Your creditors move in like vultures putting unnecessary
strain on a situation of which you have no control.
People give advice and oh are they full of advice.
Yet you remain alone and shattered behind closed doors.
After a very long time,
you suddenly notice the beauty of nature again.
A beautiful flower, a dragonfly buzzing over your head.
Then you realize that spirit has always been with you.
Slowly you start to restore your faith.
Then a virus strikes unannounced.
People became desperate and destructive with their actions,
manners, and words.
Those who once showed compassion towards you
turn into little gremlins and distance themselves.
Again you're knocked down, what now, where to next?
But your hands remain tied, your faith remains challenged.
The days roll into weeks, the weeks into months.
The virus isn't making things easier to find employment.
Everything has changed and you have to find a way to adapt
The question remains how.
As soon as you think you found a break, the rug gets
pulled out from under you yet again.
Your speak to the spirit, say your daily prayers and
try to remain positive.
Your fingers already raw from desperately clinging onto the

side of the sinking boat.
I pray for things to change, to improve.
Circumstances always change for the better they say!
I must just keep on believing
that something better is around the corner.
Something tailored made just for me.
Until then I'll remain in the shadow within.

Lindi Baird

EMILY JAMES

YOU DID NOT BREAK ME

An unplanned pregnancy
A child that went unnoticed
A teenager hidden away,
finding a quiet place in the pages of her imagination
A woman knowing the world was passing her by
A wife watching the seasons change from a locked window
A mother living with the fear and mess he left behind
And then the winds of change blew...

I found my strength
I learned my worth
I may have fallen but I never stayed down
I may have struggled but I refused to quit
I walked broken roads with my bare feet bleeding but I never stopped
I will never stop

I stand here today strong
I stand here knowing what I'm capable of
I have risen from the hell that my past tried to keep me in and I will
continue to rise until I reach the heavens

Life did not break me
You did not break me

Emily James

SHE ROSE

She rose
The world tried to break her
It almost did
She rose

Against the odds
Despite what they said
With dirt on her face
And blood under her nails
She rose

Like a phoenix under a star-filled sky
She rose

Emily James

ROBBIE J SHERRAH

IN THE ANTIQUITIES OF HER DREAMS

We were out taking a stroll along the beach; it was a quiet afternoon, and the sky was harmonious blue like the water. She was barefoot and poking about into the sand with a stick, looking for fossils that she adored to collect.

"You know not many people think about fossils, I think they're amazing, they're history frozen in time. They remind me of stories of little creatures that suddenly stopped breathing at a moment's notice. If you stop and think about it, they're gifts from the past to look to the future."

She was right, fossils do tell a story, she always had a way of saying so little, however saying so much.

I knew that she kept secrets, I knew her face was sometimes a dark storybook, I knew that she rarely spoke of her father, other than once a year on her birthday when she would pull out a jewelry box that he had given her before abandoning her when she was three. She would open that box and stare at it, frozen in time, as though something had once belonged. I knew it had to be a painful memory, and I knew better not to ask of its nature.

"Oh, I think we have a good one, I'm going to wash it off and see what we've found."

Rise From Within

This one had the markings of a tiny bird, so I was surprised when she placed it gently back into the water where she had found it, so I asked her why?

"Well one night after waking from my dreams there was a wounded sparrow in my window and I decided to keep him for a friend to protect me, but I didn't know better and I kept him inside my jewelry box and he suffocated. So ever since, in the antiquities of my dreams, I made a solemn promise to all birds to never cage them again."

Robbie J Sherrah

RHAWN

A SEPARATION WITH NO PAPERS I

Last night for the first time since this COVID-19 lockdown began I drove through a checkpoint to pick up my girls from their Dad. Glaring floodlights. Army, police, and traffic controllers. A lot of men in uniforms. All that was missing was barbed-wire, rubble, and assault rifles and I would have been transported to places I've only seen on screens.

Since hearing about these checkpoints I've had an uneasiness about how "police discretion" would work for the more marginalized in our community, along with a recognition of my own privilege. Suddenly I didn't feel so confident.

"Heading home?" a young man in army fatigues.

"No, I'm going to pick up my children from their Dad."

"Court orders?"

"I don't have any."

Now I'm talking to a police officer. Explaining that no paperwork has been lodged with the courts as we have an amicable separation and worked things out between us. I'm told to pull over. I wait. I answer more questions. "No. No emails. No text messages tonight, we spoke on the phone". He is gentle, but there is a hard edge beneath the gentleness when he tells me these checkpoints have been in place for a while now, and I should know better. I tell him my ex-husband has never been asked for documents for our kids. In fairness they are only interested in the reason for travel- his has always been traveling to work, or returning home. I wait. I'm not sure if they're going to let me through. Or what the full weight of the consequences will be if they don't. I begin to reflect on how hard I worked for the kind of separation that has landed me here. A separation with no papers.

Finally, I'm cleared to go.

I'm shaken. It's been a tough day and I was tender when I set out on this last task for the day. Brimming tears distort the road ahead. Safer to let them fall.

As I drive, headlights reflecting from the trees play a movie of memories. Memories of all that led from death threats to a separation with no papers.

Rhawn

A SEPARATION WITH NO PAPERS II

I could paint you a picture of love and light. Of compassion, forgiveness, a craving for peace and harmony. Maybe if you missed the edge in my voice, the distance in my eyes I could even convince you. Yet a piece of truth can leave enough untold to echo lies.

The rest is not pretty. It's raw and messy, and dare I say mercenary. It was the gritty eyes of sleepless nights, tear-filled tantrums, grief, rage, and attendance letters for too many absences from school because mama couldn't pull herself together—again.

It was two years of painstakingly putting pieces of myself back together, after twenty years of losing myself in him. Barely enough for Sun Tzu's advice "Know thy self, know thy enemy."

It was knowing the scared little boy and the ghosts that raged within him and who was present in each interaction.

It was a huge grumpy ex-racehorse teaching me boundaries when all he wanted was breakfast.

It was choosing to go against expert advice knowing for this one a VRO would be a red rag to a bull.

It was finding out my rights and bluffing my way through; knowing damn well he wouldn't seek legal advice. It telling him where we were on my terms, rather than spending my life looking out for the tail that would lead him to us.

It was accepting that in doing so I was deemed beyond help.

It was fervent prayers for protection and accepting some things I could not bargain for.

It was remembering blacking out with his hands around my throat and a hundred other violations big and small.

It was deciding my daughters would not grow up thinking that was normal or okay. It was admitting I'd lost myself so fully I'd not found a way to leave for me.

It was kids missing their daddy. Daddy's accusations. Contemplating throwing myself in front of the train that rattled my house in the witching hour—because everything hurt so fucking bad.

It was sifting through the rubble of my marriage. Examining piece by piece to see what was mine and what I needed to discard, or return.

It was being told that in leaving I saved three lives, maybe four. And eventually believing it.

It was avoiding his triggers where I could. Sacrificing the home that had become my prison. It was treading on eggshells when I needed to, instead of every fucking day.

It was recognising I wasn't in this alone. Seeing his strengths and weakness and choosing which to feed. It was compromise upon compromise. A dash of compassion. Pain. Anger. And boundaries.

Until one day all that we'd mixed into the cauldron began to smell like freedom.

It began to look like a separation without papers.
With trembling fingers I write this, knowing there is no roadmap out. That one woman's salvation could be another's death warrant. It is my hope that anyone reading this finds the heart and an understanding that the knowing of you and yours matters.

Rhawn

NICOLE LABONTE

SWEPT AWAY

He swept me away to another world; where perfection existed, one glance of his golden eyes I believed nothing could ever hurt me again. So much loss before him, I finally believed in fairy tales. He said the perfect things, he promised me life, and I followed walking on clouds believing I would fly forever with him beside me. He slowly made me breathless; childish lies so easily caught, but his charm would take over me, swallowing me whole. I was falling deeper and deeper into darkness, but the moments I was in his arms I felt no pain.

Eventually, his mask came off; a good disguise while he crippled me, slowly, excruciatingly. He saw my scars, too pronounced to hide, using my pain and vulnerability to continuously suck me in. He tried to destroy everything I was, to rebuild himself with my broken pieces. Wanting to build his foundation from killing the soul of a good woman, a woman who loved him to the ends of the world and back, unconditionally.

Once he knew he could break me no longer; he was gone, taking every piece of me that he could. Money, my heart, my life. Left broken and bleeding on the ground, alcohol became an escape. Tears became uniform; almost homeless, I had to rise above.

I rose from the darkest depths I had ever seen before; born of fire, my spark never died. He killed pieces of me that needed to be destroyed, for abuse was something I had known to be routine. I found myself, dusted off the past, and walked towards my future.

Here I am now, without him, not only living but thriving. Stronger, better, unstoppable. He can keep the broken pieces he took from me, build himself on weakness while I make a name for myself. My name finally in print; stability for my child and myself. A piece of me will always love him; the heart can't always help who it loves, but I learned to love myself. I turned the bad into good, I will continue to fly, dreams do come true.

Nicole Labonte

SHARMANI T. ADDERLY

MENDACITY

He kinda just happened
Yeah
He swept in outta nowhere
His smile was beguiling
His energy was addictive
He brought heat to her cold
And
In her dry parched soil
He planted a seed
And it took hold

She wasn't looking for him
Definitely not
But lost in the darkness
He found her
He took her hand
Led her to the light
And she let him
His strength refreshing
His mind intriguing
His aura became
Her answer
His seedling anchored root

His eyes were fireflies

Where there was dusk
He brought light
Where there was monotony
He sparked excitement
Once dry barren fields
No longer existed
Now,
Green, lush fauna thrived
Leaves danced at the sound
Of his voice
She found hope in his embrace
His seedling grew a stem

She took him to corners
Of her garden
Where no feet had walked
Fences overgrown
Paths wild with brush
She wanted him to know
She pulled back her skirt
And exposed her scars
He could've critiqued,
Scoffed, ran
Instead, he pruned
And patched
And watered
His seeding grew branches

Together,
They lay on soft green thick grass

His lips kissed
Her bruised tired eyes
His touch spread like ointment
Over her dry cracked emotions
His warmth
Made
The grey of her skin blush
She showed him her moon
He traced her name in stars
She let him
Read her dreams
And touch her lullaby
She saw beauty in his words
And a blanket in his arms
His seedling grew vines

She wanted him to see more
She wanted to show him
The beauty behind her pain
The cool, soothing waterfalls
Exhilarating mountain peaks
Billowing meadows
But—
He didn't want to
She didn't understand
Why wouldn't he want
To share it all with her
So,
She tried again
He stifled her

She stood frozen
As his expression became
dangerous
Anger engulfed him
Dark clouds rolled in
In a flash of lightning
The beautiful rhythm of his
Voice
Now boomed like menacing thunder
His storm blocked the sun
The Leaves trembled
A chill permeated the air
Her stars began to fall from the sky
Like the rain falling from her eyes
His vines grew thorns

His shadow became Herculean
Tender lips now grimaced
Viciously with anger
His bare teeth glistened
His breath like growls of rage
Made the earth shake
Gentle hands became fists of
Claws
And
Without warning
He thrashed through her gardens
Mercilessly
Uprooting flower beds
Plowing up well-laid fields

The large oak that once held their names
In love
On its trunk
He chopped
And shredded
With bare hands
She stood paralyzed
In fear
And pain
Who was this monster?
What happened to his warmth?
His heart?
She couldn't move-
She couldn't save herself
So
He ran over her
His thorns slicing deep into her
She bled profusely

Somehow
She found the strength
To crawl away
And sought refuge
beneath a large branch
Of the broken oak tree
She looked up at the darkened sky
Finding herself once again
Lost in the agonizing darkness
She lay still
She was sliced from the inside out

The life seeping out of her
Returning to the earth
She gasped softly
Praying the monster
Wouldn't hear her
Find her
To finish her off
She lay still
It hurt too much to move
She could hear him screaming her name
He was blaming her for the carnage
And she prayed
To die in peace
Alone
That his seedling
May die also

Sharmani T. Adderley

DISGUISED

Delicate are the wonders
That bring me joy
Minute the baubles that
Supply me with pleasure
When fantasy tastes so much
Better than reality
The depth of contentment
Stands far too deep to measure
But no one believes this...

Fragile is the tightrope that I walk
But no one sees this...
A fine unsteady line between light
And darkness
The darkness is deep
It's frightening
Void of buoyancy
The darkness vacuums and sucks in
Making it near impossible to emerge
The darkness is agonizing
An abyss of anger and hostility
Impatience and depression

Thus the choice is obvious
To dwell vivaciously in the light
The sound of birds
The warmth of family and friends
Sunshine and sunsets

Rise From Within

Sparkling blue oceans
The laughter of children
Champagne bubbles
Blue skies and even rain

You awake each day with the darkness
Yapping at your heels
Beckoning you to veer
Close enough to the edge
Just close enough for its tentacles
To snake around your ankles
And drag you into its cold dank lair

And you awake each day
Walking that tightrope a bit stronger
Willing body and mind
Each day your smile broader than before
You try to touch others positively to make the light
Radiate brighter
You choose words of icing and sprinkles
To taste better in the ear
Rather than lie still
And allow the darkness to feast on
Your laziness,
Your weakness,
You fight for the light

When along comes the darkness
No longer an engulfing, permeating mass
It has taken shape and form

It's disguised itself in clothes
Because the harder you fight
The more deceptive it becomes
Each time the voice and form are different
But you know it...

Sometimes, it's disguised
To discredit your energy
No matter how hard you work
How early you show up
Or how late you leave
How sick you come and perform
It tells you to do more, be more!
You're just not up to standard
It grades and degrades you, it evaluates you
Often unfairly
It rates and berates you
It advances others over your talent and
Dedication
It amplifies the minuscule flaws
And ignores the magnificence of your
Progress
Still, you walk tall on your tightrope never looking down

So
The darkness attacks your galaxy
It tells those around you that your words are fake, disingenuous, lies
Your smile is counterfeit
And that your light is artificial
Your walk is haughty

Rise From Within

Your style is unacceptable
Your desire to not conform, confirms your conceit
And little by little the people begin to buy into the darkness
Those people, they don't know how excruciatingly hard it is for you
to keep the lights on
That you breathe light out
Because you need it to breathe back in
They just don't know how hard you
Searched to find you, to be you
Authentically you, comfortable you
The you that can compliment, support,
Uplift, and enrich with the purest sincerity
Those people that you bolstered, listened to,
Prayed for and with, cried with, even fed
Those people you loved
Rather than stand by you in the light, in the
Laughter, in the warmth
Instead gravitated obligingly to the frigid
Evil darkness

You've been in that darkness
Many times before
You know the danger
You have the stitches
Some wounds will never heal
Some are cut way too deep
You've been stifled and strangled
Many times you almost didn't make it out
You almost gave in, you almost gave up
It's so much easier to surrender to it

And let it feast on your mind
Control your thoughts and actions
Staying in the light is the fight
But the rewards are far greater
The fruit far sweeter

So understand that
Because of my light
The smile I wear is from a gratified place
A place of peace
A harmony God carved into the chambers
Of my existence
The tranquility I exude is the prize from the
Wars I've fought and won
My words of milk and honey were birthed
From the stinging verbal assaults lashed
(Un)Consciously at me for being me
My walk is my victory dance
A touchdown to the elements that I hurdled
Over to get here
My style is authentically me, as I envision Me
And I conform not to the cages built-in clone images
But to the freedom and joy that comes with
Standing in the light...

So when I reached out to you
My embrace, I endeavoured would be an adhesive
I hoped to piece you back together,
Bandage you up and spur you on
So that you fight a little harder

A little longer
And way stronger

I know what it must seem like, but
There is joy when you emerge from the darkness
And I will you to want it
To see it
Give yourself a chance to
Enjoy it
Embrace it
Appreciate it
And realize the fight is worth it if you just
Don't look
Down into the darkness

Sharmani T. Adderley

SHAWNA OLIBAMOYO

A BRUSH WITH THE DARK

She was there in what seemed to be a dream
Slowly losing herself in the midst of chaos
Feeling trapped in her own chains of doubt
Tangled in a web that seemed never to unwind
The pain she felt within her heart was deep
Like a thorn to her side
Sadness taking over
Leading to a coma of fear
That brushed across her spine
Would she find strength and courage
Or allow the fall to keep her down?
Desperately wanting peace within her soul
That magical place that she once knew
Of happiness love and gratitude
She would not give in to the darkness
But instead
Stood up
To begin the journey on the path that was unclear
Determined to finding her way
Lead by the power of the light
That shone down from above

Shawna Olibamoyo

VALERIE GOMEZ

I'M NOT DEAD

I`ve been held hostage for almost as long as I lived.
A dark past has got me trapped in my head,
and the closest I get to freedom is by my pen.
My ink consists of the blood of my own anxious heart,
and the fucken audience who wish to do me harm.
I`m not free, especially from sin.
I bask in the ink of pretty bloody red
because nobody can see my pain, and that means it doesn`t exist.
I`m full of shit.
I`m fucken full of shit!
I`m fucken worthless…
And all I can get myself to do regularly is scream by my pen.
What everyone sees as bitching is my therapy.
I`m only half living, but they will never see.
Liquid salt runs freely, and I can`t swim.
I`m drowning slowly, but I`ll never stop kicking.
Emotional drama queen, that`s me.
Mania and rage have me twisted, but you`d never guess…
I`m gonna look so damn cute bathing in your warm red.
No, I`m not free, not even close…
All I can do is write shit down, and hope I don't explode…
I can`t deal with my past, but I refuse to make any more ghosts.
You might not like my words, but it`s my life I`m writing about,
and this is the sound of my voice.
Call me what you want as you read my words.

You think I`m getting nowhere, but I`m being heard.
You couldn`t silence me if you were blind,
because my writing isn't about you or your judgement…
It`s about how I heal myself.

Valerie Gomez

SURVIVING THE MOMENT

Somethings are meant for letting go.
While others are meant to be slain and buried over and over again.
I`ll take that shit to the trees…
So don't try to tell me which deserves which.
My demons are mine be it dead or alive.
Don't try and tell me the past can`t hurt.
The future isn't even here and that shit already hurts too.
I`m barely living, but I`m still here,
so don`t fucken tell me how I`m supposed to live.
I might be a mess, but I got this.
I`m going to continue taking it day by day, even if I have to sleep
with murder nightmares and fuck life daydreams.
This is how I fight.
This is how I`m surviving.

Valerie Gomez

VERA E. VALENTINE

AWAKENING

I woke,
With an intense burning inside,
As though my body was ablaze,
Beneath my skin.

I am finally transforming into the Phoenix;
The one smoldering,
The one sleeping within.

Vera E. Valentine

RISE

You lash out at me for having feelings.
You punish me, for using my voice.
You take away my power, by using silence: like strings on a puppet.

But darlin',
I've been here before;
And I deserve to speak,
Be heard,
Be seen.

I've fought, til' I was bloodied and broken;
Yet I still stand in my own light,
And your cruelty will not defeat me.

Vera E. Valentine

S.L. HEATON

I WILL RISE

I was lying flat on my back
in the middle of a place called rock bottom
and through the tears, I saw it
one small ray of light
and beyond the screams of why
I heard it
a faint whisper of hope
I will forever be searching for a reason to believe
because you see
falling down has always been my forte
but staying down will never be my style
I will rise--over and over again

S.L. Heaton

ALL AT ONCE

Your words reduced her existence to a shameful insignificance as if she had been lying to herself about who she thought she really was, to the person who truly knows her heart. When the truth of the matter is, you never knew her at all but tried to distort her into a perversion of the woman she actually is. You crossed lines as though they never existed, disrespecting her each and every step of the way until there was no turning back. You should know this she is stronger now, and she will never again allow the words that fly from an irrelevant, snarling mouth to have any effect, whatsoever, on her worth. You will never again have that kind of power.

S.L. Heaton

J VERONICA CHRISTOPHERSON

NEW

This new me- she remembers
The Love that came before
each excruciating heartbreak
The shared joy and dreams
The laughter, the reasons
And she feels- even now- the breaking and tears that accompanied
The vicious soul tearing
Each crack, each fissure filling with red hot pain
She remembers- the begging for understanding
With no answers to be found
Until the day- It no longer mattered
She remembered herself
And a whole new love began
This new woman- she remembers
But she doesn't live there anymore
She is too busy following
Her light and lust for Life
Bringing to herself new dreams and paths untraveled

J Veronica Christopherson

STRENGTH

Should you see me fall apart
Please, do not pity me-
for life has taught me
to be VERY strong indeed
Not the first, nor I surmise, the last
That my Soul demanded to breathe
So- don't judge, nor gossip
Because you will find; believe me ;}
In your not-so-wise 'wisdom'
That once again, you've underestimated me
For that 'Falling apart' you witnessed
That made you laugh and preen...
Is just my Heart and Soul gearing up
For the next mountain I will climb!

J Veronica Christopherson

ZEN GAFSHA

THE WOMB OF THE HEART

Grief is the price we pay for love. No matter how much currency we pay with; our hearts can remain empty. It is a tragedy to bury a child but the heartbreak of losing one's first son whilst still pregnant with him is indescribable. My life was colored with the happiness of the impending arrival of my son but he drew his last breath at only 5 months gestation. Following a series of pain I chose to ignore, my waters broke at midnight on the 19 January 2005, my heart pauses every time I speak this date, the same way for a year after my loss, every month remained January in my mind – my world could not move beyond the callous hand fate had dealt me.

When the words of supposed comfort came I found only rage, a blinding rage against all who tried to offer my broken heart solace. No one tells you how grief is a concoction of things and not a single dose of a known substance. I recall the pitiful girl, shook to the core, tracing her fingers across the face of a baby in a magazine trying to kindle what it would be like to hold her child. The cold page gave little refuge, the wretched sobs wracked my body, wailing like a wounded animal from a visceral pain that gripped me. Helplessness gave way to hate - for myself, anger for mothers, abandonment by the baby, panic attacks when seeing babies and pregnant people, even on television. I had sunk to the depths of despair. I imploded albeit silently. I was ashamed of my flaw, the incompetent cervix that cost my son his life, that turned my womb into a grave with the simple words on a scan report "there is a single foetus in breach position, 20 weeks gestation, there is no heartbeat and intra-uterine death is confirmed". A medical conclusion after 48 hours whilst they made me wait for my son to die inside me, I was made to hear his fading heartbeat, a merciless requirement. The reality of this single sentence marred my naive dreams.

In my darkest hours, I felt like the light in my soul had vanished and all the good I ever was, was gone. When there is the death of a loved one, we usually have memories to share and mutual mourning to indulge in and this helps the healing process; but a child lost in the womb is unknown to the world as if he never were and the mother's grief is in solitude, confined only to her heart and the cells of her body that once housed her child.

I refused the antidepressants, I chose to feel everything, the churning rawness of it all. I chose to hate myself and blame myself, to feel robbed, to speak ill of God, of fate, self pity embraced me as I indulged my pain. Most women would attempt to have another child quickly but I remembered the promises I shared with my son as a person, not a thing to be replaced, not a figment of my imagination to be changed and I mourned him as I should. I gave our bond the respect it deserved.

All, however, was not lost, the other heart that once beat inside me started to rekindle its light slowly in silence, my child came to me, in my thoughts, in my dreams he gave me courage and placed in my hand my only known retreat – my notebook. "Remember me," he said "not just the last few hours on this earth, that was not my life, that is not yours either" he whispered. His voice became my encouragement. Deep within I knew my dying heart conjured my survival instinct by creating him as part of the fabric of my conscience. "Write to me mama, write for me, the way you did before I was even a line on a pregnancy test" I recalled my letters to him in fondness, after a long time a smile reached my eyes. There was hope. I felt guilty to feel it but it warmed the embers of my heart.

I found emancipation through my penned words. I wrote daily, I spoke to me, I spoke to him and I learnt to extend myself to the suffering of others and gratitude for the time we shared. Slowly, I started to accept my life was forever changed by loss but I was made kinder for it, there was a purpose to my pain. I acknowledged him when people asked if I had children and the sting of the words started to feel less corrosive, the more I revived him. I will always bear the scars of heartache at losing him, the cracks on the mountain that I am, now succumb to certain anxieties and the peaks and troughs of depression. I clamber out of the darkness as his spirit propels me forward, I can navigate my way back to the surface. The love we shared is that compass directing me toward the light every time I find myself on my knees because "My Immortal" by Evanescence was on the radio, or my hands fall onto the little teddy his father had bought with hopeful eyes that his son would one day hold.

I fell but I rose, from within, the fire that remained from him spurring me on. The strength he possessed, even fighting for his life for 48 hours with no waters to sustain him, baffled doctors; but that strength flows in me too. How could I let that die? I could succumb to my wounds or I could let him shine through by getting up again. Every, single, time, past the fear, past the insecurity and challenges that lay forth in my journey of giving life to his brothers that followed. Hearts beat once again in a blighted place, an empty womb revived and empty arms were filled. I am stronger and fiercer, fate cannot pluck my daring heart anymore; it may shatter but my pieces are like droplets of water that inevitably enjoin and I survive. A bereaved mother is a force beyond reckoning and I have delved into this abyss with other women, I have shared my strength and invoked theirs; this I resolved was my reason for suffering – I would raise other women when their grief shackled them, I would let the great love I shared with my son wither to nothing.

My realisation that I was his only ambassador in this world drove me to reach into my life force and find the love and happiness he gave me to share with others. "Remember me," he said "And you will remember you" I would give life to his memory. I would speak his name and count him amongst my kin, I was made to go on without him but I would be damned if people did not come to know my son whose heart is eternal for me.

For him, I lived, through me, he survives.

Zen Gafsha

ERI RHODES

FIANNA

The kind of girls and women I admire are fiercely, unabashedly, unapologetically, and wholly, themselves. They know the world is a harsh and bitter place, but they also know that they are stunning, lovely, striking in their authenticity. These women are fighters in the war against fakery and artifice, against fraud and insincerity. They are the brave soldiers against sanctimonious bigotry and hypocritical judgment. You will never beat these warriors with insults or criticism. You see, they've done this before. Every day they put on their armor to take a stand for integrity. From my tribe of wildly eccentric, recklessly loving, and passionately unconventional characters I have learned more than I could ever hope to from books, wise men, counselors, or professors.

Eri Rhodes

I FORGIVE YOU

I looked into the face of the broken girl in the broken mirror. I stared deep into red-rimmed eyes and watched as tear-filled memories ran down my face. "I am so sorry", I told that child in the mirror. I wanted to do right by her after letting her be mistreated for so damn long. But I didn't know what to say so I said I was sorry and that I would try again another day. Then I washed my face and turned away from the broken girl in the broken mirror.

I looked into the face of the broken spirit in the broken mirror. I stared at dark purple eyes and reached up to untangle hair matted with blood. "This is the last time ", I told the spirit in the mirror. Promises had been made and broken before, so this one had better count. I didn't know how to leave, but I knew I was going to try. I cleaned my matted hair and turned away from the broken spirit in the broken mirror.

I looked into the eyes of the broken face in the broken mirror. I stared intently, searching for proof of life. "Is anybody in there?", I asked the woeful eyes in the mirror. Cheerless, ghostly, and forsaken, the blue eyes stared back at who I used to be. I licked my lips, tried to speak, then gave up and turned away from the broken eyes in the broken mirror.

I looked into the smiling face of the warrior in the broken mirror. I reached up and touched the edges of my smile, felt my way over wrinkles and laugh lines. "I did it!" I told the fighter in the mirror. I had gone to war for the child and the spirit and the life in my eyes. I had saved us all from the destructive forces in the universe.

Apologies and forgiveness are unnecessary now as I stare at the fiery and fearless warrior in the broken mirror.

Eri Rhodes

FIJA CALLAGHAN

FALSE BRICK ROAD

I've known scarecrows and I've known men
With hearts encased behind tin walls,
Black and calloused with disuse;
With limbs of straw that felt no pain,
Although the flicker of a flame
Was enough to send them screaming.
And though I live in terror of
The silence in this emerald cage,
Still, I can look down, down, down
At that false brick road, and know
That they were cowards
And I was brave.

Fija Callaghan

IN SHADOWS

Although I walk in shadow still
and sleep entwined in snares and thorns,
and wrap myself in thistle-silk
against the wind's incessant scorn,
though the storms of summer rage
and wash the stars into the sea
to choke among the ragged weeds
and spectres of forgotten dreams —

Still, along these lonely roads
of yellow brick and bloody glass,
I extend my hand into the gale
and ask the tempest for a dance.

Fija Callaghan

H.R. CURRIE

FORESIGHT AND FOOTING

The sounds of nature lulled her into apathy for all but the beauty of her surroundings, while pine needles tangled like ornaments of failure into windswept hair as she lay upon the forest floor—numb to the pain and averting her eyes from which parts of her might be bleeding or broken from the fall.

As she stared up through the canopy, drawn into the deep blue of a cloudless sky, she worked to focus on the depth that she knew evaded her eyes.

She could remember doing this as a child– imagining miles of atmosphere for as long as her focus would hold until it was inevitably pulled back to the illusion of a single layer. Slowly, soreness and sting rose to the surface to ruin the illusion of serenity, as well.

She still could not bring herself to look for breaks that she could not yet feel, choosing instead to ignore this likely reality for as long as possible.

As she anxiously waited for a rush of agony to work its way through the shock, she bent her fingers and wiggled her toes, counting each one until she was sure that they all remained unscathed. She moved on, gingerly moving every inch of her body, some parts easier than others, taking inventory by feel— finally realizing that the blinding pain she'd been expecting would not come.

There was pain, but nothing that she could not handle.

As she slowly pulled herself to her feet, appreciating how light and shadow danced as one throughout the forest, the weight of her survival flooded her mind with the images, sounds, and terror of her fall.

She quickly forced these images out of her mind as she realized that she still remained lost and alone with no bearing—choosing not to dwell upon failure and focusing instead on her fresh knowledge of foresight and footing.

With no time to waste, she steadied her breathing as she looked around for the next tree to climb.

H.R. Currie

RIVER STAGE

Above the arch of her secret bridge, she lies on dusty timber. With feet and unaccompanied melodies dangling over water she barely noticed flowing freely underneath, her smile overtook as song and sun fell into harmony with her soul.

For one who craved simplicity as much as a companionship matching the breeze dancing through her hair, she could not deny that her truest peace had always been found in the former. When a golden sun and amber leaves could spark such a staggering passion, an ounce of reality was easily deafening to someone like her, despite the hunger for a stirring chorus.

But it was here that she found her cadence, lying on her secret bridge. She thought back to every bend and stepping stone she had stumbled through to find this place to simply be. This place taught her that true bridges were never made for burning and embankments came with many faces, but her solos could rise above water and wind to always sing her home.

This was her place of still and song, where she'd always find a freedom to write the score.

H.R. Currie

KELLI J GAVIN

FOLLOW

I asked you to follow
You wanted to lead
I couldn't remember where we were going
It didn't matter
You knew the way
The path seems to have changed
The road seems to stray
I don't need direction
I needed the desire to go
To lead
To walk
To move
Forward
One foot in front of the other
Stay where you are
I am ready to do this on my own

Kelli J Gavin

THE ROAD HOME

I have walked one too many roads
A few stray paths have distracted me
Not always sure where I was going
Or why I was called away
Home should be where the heart is
But sometimes my heart would fail
A faulty human with a messy soul
At least I thought I should search
Maybe there was something more
Someplace where my mind could rest
Where I wouldn't feel such constant flux
A place where sleep would come easily
But those roads lead to nothing I wanted
Everything I thought was for me- wasn't
Joy couldn't be found down any worn road
Happiness couldn't be detected on a new path
Rest was absent from any trail my feet tread
Boldness was needed to turn back around
To return to where I had come from
I wasn't going to accept how I had failed
I learned that acceptance was defeat
Finding the strength to make changes
Discovering new ways of loving life daily
The road home seemed to be a needed journey
I realized that I needed to be elsewhere
Only to find that road home
I needed to create a new life

Rise From Within

This time I will stay the course and rediscover
That everything I need is already within reach
The road home is the only road for me

Kelli J Gavin

L.E

HOPE

Write about hope they said. What do I know about hope? I know pain, I know anger, I know lust, I even know envy. What do I know about hope? Hope is the flickering candle flame that we move towards because we're afraid of the dark. Hope is the huddled child in the corner, begging for their mother.

Hope is the mother on her knees praying to a God she isn't sure is still listening to her, or if he ever did. Hope is saying yes when he pops the question because you know you're marrying potential. Hope is the belief that you love him enough for the both of you.

Hope is flushing the pills, putting the bottle down, pulling the needle out of your arm, or the gun out of your mouth. Hope is putting your feet on the floor, instead of pulling the blankets over your head. Hope is the twenty seconds of courage in the face of overwhelming odds that no matter what you do, life is going to kick you in the teeth and send you reeling. Hope. What do I know of hope?

L.E.

I RISE

When I was ten, my most precious treasure was my teddy bear. His name was Teddy and he comforted me and caught many of my tears as I clutched him to my chest. When I was twenty-four, I treasured no single thing more than my simple golden wedding band. At thirty-five, my children gave me a coffee cup and a cheap plastic mood ring for Mother's Day. These became my most favorite possessions. I still wear that ring – and it still turns my finger green.

I was forty before I realized that my most precious possession was never a thing. It was my own strength. Through all the tragedies in my life – the loss, heartbreak, the utter chaos, and madness – I still rise.

I have lost much in my life and the grief is a constant companion. I know that I will never be able to regain the simple naivete that I once viewed the world through – and this, more than anything, is my greatest regret. The loss of my own innocence.

On the bad days, I begin to doubt my own self-worth. I doubt my reason for being. I doubt my place in this world. I lose myself in my own self-deprecation and fear. And then the sun comes up, the clouds clear, and I rise.

My strength is my most prized possession.

L.E.

MANDY KOCSIS

CROWN

I sold my dreams for pennies
You bought them for free
And when you didn't want them
Gave them back to me
In tears, I started building
With rage I made them grow
Now my dreams are priceless
I wouldn't barter them for gold
You couldn't see my vision
Completely missed my strength
And the fact that I was flying
Because you couldn't see my wings
Now you're lost in the rubble
Of the world that you brought down
While I'm flying high above you
With my kingdom for a crown.

Mandy Kocsis

ON MY OWN

I look at our past
Who I was with you
And how I've evolved
Since "us" just fell through
Literally, everything's different
Nothing's the same
But who I am, now
Is what's most rearranged
And I've got to say
This version is better
I'm vibrating higher
Right down to the letter
I might still be darkness
But, my God, how I shine
And I might be broken
But I'm still divine
So when you look back
Years on from now
Know the best thing that happened
Was you walking out
I thank you for that
From the depths of my soul
In that moment, I shattered
And became beautifully whole
And the best part? I did it
All on my own.

~Mandy Kocsis

LYSSA DAMON

ETERNAL FLAME

Jonathan Keet shuffled off this mortal coil on a Wednesday afternoon, three days shy of his eighty-ninth birthday.

Logan found himself on a road trip to the old boy's funeral. How fitting that he should be making this trip in Selena, the 1962 Mercedes-Benz 190-SL gifted to him by his grandfather last Christmas.

"I know you'll treasure her as I always have."

Grandad had named his car after the love of his life. Selena, the grandmother Logan never got to meet, although he knew her through the many stories Grandpa told. Logan smiled, thinking that grandpa was finally with his beloved again.

'My Selena's eyes were as blue as the car, that's how they came to share a name.' My two goddesses.

Gran and Grandpa married in 1962. They bought the car that same year. Years passed. A son. Two daughters, eight grandchildren, one grandson - born last, three months after Selena died.

The road was long, but there was little traffic and Selena was filled with memories. She smelled of leather, cherry, and maple pipe tobacco. Logan didn't smoke but he kept a pouch of Grandpa's tobacco in the glove compartment. He breathed deeply and replayed the many hours spent with grandpa, chatting, polishing the vintage beauty, and drinking cola out of glass bottles.

So many years ago. Before life happened and Logan only saw Grandpa at family gatherings. Even more seldom since Logan and Gail's divorce. Grandpa believed in the magic of true love. Logan no longer did.

'Callie Inn'
He followed the signs and pulled up outside just as dusk turned to darkness. Selena looked every bit the elegant grande dame parked outside the quaint stone building.

The interior of the inn, just as beautiful as the outside. A curry dinner - Grandpa's favourite. An after-dinner whiskey.
"Cheers Grandpa. I hope you find your Selena."
A good night's rest. He dreamed of Grandpa.

Breakfast was delicious. Logan noticed a couple at the next table, obviously in love. He overheard snippets of conversation. 'Honeymoon', 'Forever'. As he got up, the young man called to him. "Excuse me Sir, is that your car out front?"

The couple asked for a few photos of them in the car, a honeymoon keepsake after a long separation. Logan obliged a few happy snaps. Some on his phone, some on a beautiful vintage camera the young man had. The young couple's love was evident. It almost made him forget that love didn't exist.

Soon enough, Logan was on his way.

It was a rare occasion that the family came together. That evening, Logan and his mom leafed through piles of photos that Mom had found stashed away. Photos his mother had not seen in decades. "I just assumed they'd been lost in the fire."

The house fire shortly after Selena's death had stolen many memories.

A faded photo caught his eye. His car parked in front of...could it be? The sign confirmed it. Callie Inn. He flipped the photo over. 'Honeymoon". The next photo made him catch his breath. Grandpa and Grandma. Fresh-faced, smiling. Familiar.

He pulled out his phone.
"Aaaah grandpa, you found her."

Lyssa Damon

RISING HOPE

It was a sweltering summer day the Tuesday we buried you. I wore hot tears and a fake smile. Everyone telling me how sorry they were and me swallowing the angry words I wanted to say. Instead, I whispered my thanks. You abandoned me. You abandoned us.

The ceremony was beautiful, or so they tell me. It's all a blur. Men in uniform. That uniform stole you from me. From us. A perfectly folded flag. That is all I have left of you. That and Onyx.

I remember that crisp autumn day I met you. Me, quietly reading on that bench under the tree. My peaceful afternoon ruined by a goofy black dog bounding into piles of leaves and a cute marine laughing at his antics. I miss that laugh. I miss you.

I daresay Onyx misses you more than I do. My heart still aches when I remember his face the day of your funeral. He lay by the door as if waiting for you to come home. I knew he knew you weren't coming back. He didn't wag his tail. He hasn't since.

I'm not sure Onyx ever forgave me for falling in love with you. He was always your dog. Never ours. He chewed on my shoes. Ate several pairs of socks. I forgave him for peeing on my wedding dress, but only because it was three days before the wedding and the cleaners fixed his mess.

We married in autumn. Exactly a year after that first meeting. Our fairytale wedding. Our very own happily ever after. A few weeks after our first anniversary, you left. So dapper in your uniform. We

106

were so happy. I wish I had held you longer. Kissed you one more time before you left for the airport.

Summer is nearly over. My belly is round. Our daughter will be making her appearance any day. You were so excited when I delivered the news over our weekly video call. I miss you. I'll tell her about her daddy. The man I will love for eternity. My joy at becoming a mother carries the heaviness of your absence every day.

Onyx has spent every night since we lost you lying by the front door. Tonight, he was not there. He didn't come when I called. It must be the hormones because I heard my voice get high and shrill. I called and called. Nothing. I have never felt so alone.

So I'm here. In the nursery, talking to you. Waiting for the Onyx to come home.
I've not spoken to God since the day they told me you died.
Tonight I pleaded with him: "Please, I can't lose them both."

I am roused from my sleep just as the sun is rising. I am still here in the rocking chair, after rocking for hours. Waiting for Onyx to come back. Wondering if our daughter will have your eyes.

I am aware that I am not alone in the room. Onyx nuzzles my belly. A strong kick is her reply. He wags his tail whines softly and for the first time, I know that we are going to be okay.

Lyssa Damon

GYPSY'S REVERIE

SPRING

Spring. I don't know if I have ever been so grateful for its coming. The most recent season of my life has been a cold, dark, and stormy one--characteristic of Winter in every sense. I found I could no longer endure the frigidity and lifelessness of that winter with its seemingly endless night, and struck out into the darkness in search of a little starlight. I became as a vessel pitched about within a tempest in uncharted waters; winds of change and tides of destiny tumbling me about with nary a compass nor map to guide me through the precarious seas.

The dawn of a new day has seen me safely cast upon the shores of a new land and future, wild and unknown, but alive with possibilities and a stark contrast to the desolate winter I have left behind. Turning myself to face the sun, I feel the chill of the wintry past leave my bones as I begin to thaw, returning to life once again. Just as Spring has returned, heralded by new life and endless potential, so too am I renewed and inspired to trod the path that lies before me--to create a future brimming with hope, love, passion, and joy. Thus, I steel myself to embark, frolicking, upon the road less traveled toward the life that I shall painstakingly and lovingly craft. But until I have discovered how and where to build my nest, I am content to explore this unknown world with a gypsy's soul: reveling in its beauty, pausing to enjoy the wildflowers and to celebrate the songs of Spring. For Winter is finally over and behind me; the embers within me have sparked into a new flame as I leave the shores of the past behind and throw myself into the heart of this new place and my future life.

And if you wish to keep me company,
I reach out my open hand invitingly:
My journey is far from over,
And though I know not where it may lead--
If you find you have the courage,
Take my hand; come dance with me...

Gypsy's Reverie

ASCENDED FROM ASHES

I started a songbird
with a sweet melody.
A joyful song in my soul,
I was happy and free.

One day my life merged with another;
I dreamt of creating a new harmony...
Instead, expectations and plans created a cage
that had been carefully crafted for me.

Years of neglect stole the song from my soul
and I forgot the feeling of free.
Denial insisted this cage was where I belonged,

Fearing the truth of my captivity.

So I polished and gilded the bars till they shined,
trapped without hope in my sorrow.
Silent and lonely, my dreams were long gone;
I began to care not for tomorrow.

Now only a shell of my former self,
An ornament abandoned to rust,
Unsure that existing could be something more,
Bereft of love, direction, and trust.

Then I was reminded of my soul's forgotten song;
memory beckoning to me.
Pointed out that I had the key all along.
Only I could set myself free...

Free from the prison my life had become:
A cage built of lies that "should be";
Free, if only I faced all my fears,
The path to freedom lied within me.

Doubt was at war with my soul's deepest longing,
Knowing to stay meant I would not survive;
I gazed at the sky through new eyes
full of hope--
Determined, at long last, to thrive.

I struck the match, setting fire to my cage,
Liberty at the cost of destruction.

The life I had built, an inferno of pain
giving way to new freedom and passion.

The wild heart inside me began to soar
before I could take to the skies,
Finally able to break free from this life
which was built out of heartache and lies.

I glance at my gilded prison in flames;
All around me blazes and crashes.
And now, as the Phoenix, I have become,
I rise: Ascended from Ashes.

Gypsy's Reverie

THE EDGE

It all came down to this moment.
Standing on the edge of the Unknown,
The chasm of an unseen future just beyond her feet.
A leap of faith was required.

Returning to the life she had before would surely be her soul's death;
Moving forward was the only way.
Determined to survive, she squared herself--
Toes on the ledge, prepared to cast herself into a new life.

And so she risked it all.
Leaving the safety and security of her known world,
She hurtled headlong into the abyss.
Rather than free-falling into the dark and dangerous depths she feared
to be awaiting her in the spaces beyond,
She instead discovered the strength she had gained from her fight for
survival.

She realized that Fear had been her anchor to that life;
Her desperate act of courage in jumping from the precipice of her
known world and former life severed those bonds irrevocably.
And once free of that burden, she learned she was no longer weighted
to the ground.

Neither fear nor gravity could hold her now.
Her choice to leap wasn't the precursor to certain destruction
Lurking in the mysterious depths of the void,
But was the catalyst required to show her she could fly.

Gypsy's Reverie

SHARIL MILLER

PASSIONATE ASHES

A charmed life she did not lead
In fact, it may have weakened a lesser breed

Like a phoenix from the ashes, she did rise
With ever-growing determination and strength in her eyes

She vowed nothing in life would drag her down
Her face always glowing with a smile rarely a frown

From the outside looking in one would never know
Keeping it to herself not letting it show

It's said that eyes are the windows to the soul
And hers were as dark as coal

But if one took the time to look deep within
Seen would be that her love of life always shines brightly never dim

Her passion for life kept her moving on
She refused to allow it to use her as a pawn

Even if at times she was brought to her knees
Her victories over life's battles always set her free

She never wore armor to protect her from life

Rise From Within

She charged head-on naming battles as challenges, not strife

Although life could have left her broken and shattered
Clothed only in rags that were worn and tattered

She chose instead to wear her scars as her best attire
A stunning dress, woven of hellfire

Sharil Miller

CLAWING MY WAY OUT

Looking deep into my soul I find
Struggles with heartache and emotional conflict in my mind
During the past two years, I've lost me
Paralyzed by feeling empty and lonely due to my grief
The essence of myself buried so deep
I had to awake from the emotional sleep
From my own darkness, I need to claw my way out
So into the universe, I raise my voice and shout
Naming 2019 as the year
As the time to silence the fear
Fear of feeling I have nothing left to give
Knowing I need not to just exist but to live
Living my life authentically, happy, and whole
Striving to reunite myself with my passions and goal
So, I reach for my paper and pen
Writing starts to flow so freely once again
My soul is now filling with pride, joy, and love
I can't help but think there is a little angelic intervention from above
I am still fighting and have a long way to go
But, I will survive and thrive, this I know
My journey is unfolding exactly as it should be
And I am once again reuniting with me

Sharil Miller

THE RADIOACTIVEANGL

SMOLDERING PHOENIX

As the years of simmering rage
Fall silently from her eyes
Trails of flames slide down her skin
And she smolders quietly for a time.
As the ground starts to quake
And the winds begin to rise
A light comes beaming out
Her phoenix takes to the skies.

the radioactivangl

TATTOO GIRL

All the darkness rises
That she seeks to keep at bay
She wants to let it out
But to shield the others
she locks it within
And every day the battle
Leaves a stain upon her skin

the radioactivangl

STEPHANIE BENNETT-HENRY

MY COMPASS

This life, it's gotten away from me more than once. I wasn't always sure I would make it, still can't believe sometimes I'm standing here now. I find myself doing a double-take, searching my own eyes for who I am now, and who I'm not. I have fallen enough to know that if my falls were my compass, I would've crossed the point of no return several years ago. When I think of the first sixteen years, I still flinch, and even now, decades later, I have made bracing for impact an Art. So, I try to paint my story sometimes with words that make the details beautiful and it was never beautiful. It was never beautiful. But I bury the ugly, shovel words over every edge until I can look back without bleeding. And maybe I fell all those times so I could perfect the rise and maybe I'm still standing now so I can hold the words, like the only compass I've ever known, and finally walk myself home. I promise not to flinch. I promise to use my own light, shine it across my whole sky, grab the words, and know I will always land exactly where I am meant to land.

Stephanie Bennett-Henry

WHAT HAPPENS NOW

What happens now, after the fall, when you pick up the pieces of who you used to be, mix each one with who you are now? It's not just changing shoes, babe. It's your life, it's that fork in the road you finally take, it's looking in the mirror without looking away. This is it. Haven't we all waited our whole lives for this? To look ahead, see our destination, and not second guess it. There's no turning back even if we wanted to, eyes on the road, babe. That rearview mirror never was worth your time, look up. Your whole heart knows the way. Even the cracked parts, especially the cracked parts. Run your fingers over every scar, like a map, be grateful for the lessons that got you here, say goodbye to every version of yourself that fell with you and taught you how to rise. Here you are now, a hundred pieces of who you used to be, a mosaic of dead ends and lessons, blood and tears, and this version of me I recognize now that says, I am so brave with all these scars that taught me who I am, what I'm made of, and yes... I am beautiful. We are beautiful. All of us who fell a hundred times and never stayed down. I see every rise like a prayer with our names, hallelujah written in the sky as the stars come together, our wishes fall back to us, like snowflakes on our tongues, and we fall again just to go through the process of climbing back up. That fork in the road is beautiful and I am certain now of who I am and who I'm not.

Stephanie Bennett-Henry

SUEANN SUMMERS GRIESSLER

A WALK WITH DEATH

We walked along,
just Death and I.
Trailing behind me was a gossamer train,
both weightless, and yet replete with such
agonizing emblems of the horrors survived;
thorns and sutures, ashes and embers,
leaving a wispy wake as we continued on our path.

Winged memories in flight,
as fine as gold silk threads,
danced about my head and shoulders,
some with a firm grasp at the hem of my skirts,
pulling me ever forward.

This display of hope darkened Death's demeanor even more,
as did the ever-brightening dawn that
I drew us nearer to.

Death then placed a lantern in my hands,
its flame sputtering and threatening to fade out altogether;
his gift of an omen of what he feels will be.

He reveled in the withering of its nature,
his aura increasing in inky cloudiness
as only Death can.

Rise From Within

His pleasure is quickly halted,
replaced with vexation as he observes that
as I advance breezily, so, too,
does the light in my lamp, now cheerily ablaze.

As we near the end of the footpath,
the night is no longer cloaked in heavy, dark gloom.

Death stands firmly on my flowing frock to
prevent my further travel,
a sneer snaking across his features.

My gown tore away and with it,
the knifing pain, sorrow, and ailments.

My feet gained speed, chasing the dawn and light,
leaving Death to find another traveler.

I will savor my newfound strength;
I will not be continuing our journey today.

SueAnn Summers Griessler
aka The Musing Palette

LAND OF THE LIVING

What does one do when life grinds to a halt?
Daily consumption of tears
-taste the salt
New rules and restraints
Shove it down, no complaints
I've got to get back to the land of the living

Muscles are screaming, frame withers away
Betrayed by my body day after day
Summon the courage
Won't be discouraged
I will get back to the land of the living

Grasping the faintest iota of hope
Basic skills still of Herculean scope
Pain and despair
Damn you and fear
I'm joining the land of the living

Minutes to hours, days into nights
Months become years; I continue the fight
I'll forge a new path
I have faced Death's wrath
Because my life is surely worth living

Listen, I now shout this joyous refrain
Nothing for granted, will I take again
My life is revived

Yes, I have survived
Pure hope is the life I'm now giving.

SueAnn Summers Griessler
aka The Musing Palette

VAUGHN ROSTE

A SONNET

Whene're the worries of the day your attitude depress,
When bad news or harsh words you hear discourage and oppress;
When words meant to inspire you seem trite and so cliché:
"Chin up," "Take heart," "Be strong, my friend – today's a brand new day;"

When problems all surround you but solutions are unclear,
When life still throws at you its worst but yet there's more to fear;
When unanticipated loss bereaves us of what's dear,
When day begins with no real sense of hope, or joy, or cheer;

Stress threatens to engulf us, and dark mountains loom so steep,
but people tell you "just buck up" and "turn the other cheek -"
and you won't let them see you cry for fear they'll think you're weak.

Remember this, and breathe, my child, for you are not alone:
your worth is not something that you should ever have to prove.
All you need to know is that you're human, and are loved.

Vaughn Roste

WIL R.P. MCCARTHY

I HAVE FALLEN

I fell down the other day
It was a struggle
But I got back up
Sometimes it's been my own fault
My arrogance or pride
Other times I was tripped
By the mean spirits of others
Or by this thing, we call life
I've fallen a lot in my time here
I have been to dark places
Places which sap your strength
And burrow into your mind
It all still haunts me
But each time I have risen
And I will continue to rise
Rise up each time I fall again
To meet my fate
I will walk down this path
Following where it goes
To find the life
I have always wanted

Wil R.P. McCarthy

I WAS LOST ONCE

I was lost once
As I struggled to find my way
The road was covered in darkness
And my light was weak and flickering
I continued to move forward
Stumbling and falling many times
But I was determined
Every bump
Every slip
Every fall
Every pit I crawled out of
Was a lesson on how to survive
A new thing learned to watch out for
With time I found a way
To make my light shine more brightly
And now I hold it up for others to see
I know I am not alone on this road
And I hope I can help others
Find their way

Wil R.P. McCarthy

AMY PASZTAS

PHOENIX

Look deep beyond the armor
To scars upon my skin
Look way beyond the trappings
To what I hold within
See past these imperfections
The battle-scarred terrain
To bones forged out of iron
Despite the soul-deep pain
Look far beyond the number
That counts my life in years
For I am judged more justly
By adding up my tears
They do not flow too often
And never without cause
But they have made me stronger
Just like my other flaws
I faced down all my demons
Found fire in my veins
And like a phoenix rising
I swallowed down the pain
Spread wings above the fire
As I was born anew
And looked down on the battle
That raged with a reddish hue
Battle-scarred I'm stronger

Than I have ever been
A small, empathic warrior
With tattoos on her skin.

Amy Pasztas

BROKEN WINGS

Bloody, broken, beaten down
She lies upon the cold, hard ground
Her body aches, her spirit bleeds
Lost among this world of greed
Tomorrow is a brand new day
Another chance to find your way
Cut your wings, you must fit in
Remove all vestige of your sin
You are different, you are wrong
Another verse, the same old song
Cut off those wings, never fly
but deep inside her soul sobs 'why'
Years are lost while blending in
Perhaps that is the real sin
Bloody, broken, beaten down
She looks to heaven from the ground
Her wings are broken, past repair
While others laugh, and point, and stare
An anger rises in her soul
It was her wings that made her whole

Too late to fly, too much to grieve
For all this time she was deceived
The people who are all the same
Those very ones who cast the blame
Grew jealous of her fairy wings
And of the voice with which she sings
And as she laid upon the ground
Her voice cried out, a keening sound
Anger, sorrow, rage, and fear
Flowed out upon her streaming tears
And pushing up she looked around
A vengeful sprite upon the ground
She spreads the wreckage of her wings
Finally proud of broken strings
People gasp and point and stare
She laughs because she doesn't care
A day late as they like to say
Yet she has found another way
Kneeling on the bloodied earth
She feels her strength and knows her worth
Bloody, broken, beaten down
They cannot strike her from the ground
Her wings will never fold back in
She knows now they are not a sin
And looking up she starts to sing
And through the night her voice will ring
Urging those who've lost their way
To stand and fight another day...

Amy Pasztas

APRIL SPELLMEYER

BREATHING GRIEF

grief was an unwanted guest long before you were taken from me
grief would visit from time to time
whispering to me it will be a matter of time to feel its full effect
grief wanted to get to know me first
to learn what ways was the best to bring me to my knees
grief needed me to submit my will
and do as it said without question when the time came
grief was biding its time on when it would blindside me
 with no warning
that day came too soon, too fast
i crumbled
my life ripped to shreds
cries clawed their way out of throat
grief drew first blood and the final blow all at once
grief had me where it wanted me
an empty shell
a ghost to roam from room to room in search of you
grief brought baggage
sadness, heartbreak, loss, confusion, anger and thrusted it on me
i became overwhelmed
what was i to do with it all
i tried pulling them apart
taking each one aside
trying to understand

they spoke their own language
a language i would soon have to learn
pieces of me strewn in a cold world
colors faded
i was lost and alone with no rhyme or reason
all I could do was sit in silence
i did not fight grief it was easier to be an accommodating host
seconds to minutes - minutes to hours - hours to days - days to
months - months to years
every step was a somber ballet across eggshells
our home now a tomb - memories flashed - photographs face down
our song on repeat – i medicated to become numb
my will was gone
grief made me insane – i could only breathe in grief
i mourned every waking hour and slept walked through nightmares
then grief transformed to something new
i never thought possible, a new chapter began
grief and i became intimate - we became as one - our lives entwined
we finally understood each other's purpose
cohabitation became a delicate balance
now i can sit with grief
we console each other like a mother to a child
grief has become a teacher
grief has schooled me in its ways
where it's not just madness and melancholy
grief showed me to celebrate the time we shared
the family we created - memories we made - promises we swore -
eternal soulmates - undeniable love - a once upon a time - our happily
ever after put on hold until we are both among the stars
as i promised you with a pinky swear and cross my heart

i will live for you
i will live for me
i will live for us

April Spellmeyer

TRUTHS

Victim
Survivor
Warrior
Hear my truths...
Bruises hidden from the world
Blood became a familiar taste
Held down, innocence ripped away
They carved their names on my bones
Lips sewn shut to silence screams
Eyes pleading for help, never seen
Good girls do what they are told
Bad girls will feel red hot rage
Chaos became my teacher
Addiction was my best friend
A razor blade bled out my pain
Anger was my protector
Sex was my weapon of choice
Anorexia was my scale

Suicide attempts, my cries for help
Mental illnesses swung like a pendulum
Poor choices one after another
The vicious cycles kept repeating
Darkness was a warm blanket
My heart slowly becoming stone
I was a walking empty shell
A forgotten girl never meant to be
Then the day came I broke my bonds
I gave birth to my voice
Screaming no more harm will come
I burned the bridges to the past
Tended to my wounds with care
Growing a spine of steel
There is no more fear
I bathe in the light
I breathe hope
I embrace love
I am at peace
I am not a victim
I am not a survivor
I am a warrior
These are my truths...

April Spellmeyer

DEBRA MAY SILVER

BRIGHTLY COLOURED WIFE

You carry your blunt sword of sorrow
Every day and every night.
It's so worn from you drawing it ... with your fantasies of fight.

Go home to your beautiful brightly coloured wife.
She is waiting to hold you. You alone.
Before you get there take off your armour
It heavy and it's in the way of her healing your black and white soul.

The weight is too heavy to be dragging around
Find a closed corner or an open field to place your grief.
It will come to you when it needs to be felt.

Go home to your beautiful brightly coloured wife
She longs to feel you. You alone.
Not just your body but your ragged old soul.

Go hold her breathe into her being
So you can heal each other,
She needs your unguarded touch and longs to see those long lost
burning sparks back in your eyes.

She wishes for no more empty and soulless touches.. no more black
depths in her bed.

Leave your blunt sword behind, carry it no more
Leave your blunt sword behind and tell her no more lies.

Your beautiful beautiful colourful wife.
Go to her do nothing else until this you have done.
There is nothing else of importance right here and now under any moon or any sun.

Hurry... Take your black and white soul to your beautiful brightly coloured wife.

Debra May Silver

FORFEIT OF A CITY

The time I lost you, my beautiful City.

You are the one that holds all my memories stored.

My history is embedded deep in your soil
My cries still heard in the bark of your trees.

I could dig and dig for parts of my life and find them buried deep under your roads all but lost in your time.

Rise From Within

Sections of myself buried and covered in many layers of grief within
your boundaries
my beautiful lost city.

I drive past graveyards of my past, almost but not quite a different
life of mine.

These monuments of many deaths I died with no gravestone to mark
all of my passing's and losses.

These monuments of my many deaths and crucifixions.
Always from ones I loved and trusted.

No Gravestones to mark my losses and the passing of hopes that will
never be felt again.

Rusted memories, but still too sharp to bring to the surface.
So like many a graveyard that you just drive by
You briefly ponder what lies beneath the surface

But I ran from you and probably will forevermore.
but with no headstones to mark your many deaths.

Like a selfish ex-lover, I only grieve for you when I see you. My
beautiful lost city.

Debra May Silver

GYPSY MERCER

MY WARRIOR

After you
She cried
She bled
She fled
Standing tall was difficult
Her body felt defeated
Her shoulders slumped
Her smile faded
Listless
Loveless
Lost
Glassy eyed
Murmured sad speech

Until
One day
She gathered all that was left
Threw it in the air
And one stronger
Determined
Woman emerged
Her head held high
But her smile
Did not extend to her eyes
Her handshake was too strong

Her hug much too airy
She turned off
All superfluous emotion
She concentrated on survival
Denial
Winning
At any cost

They saw that she was different
And avoided her
When forced to engage
They acquiesced knowing
She no longer played by the rules of polite society
Her secrets
Her scars
She wore hidden
To ensure no target marked her again
She lost a little each day
As her warrior took over

Gypsy Mercer

MY WORDS

Long ago you stole my words
And I started using yours
It sounded natural
And I forgot the words
That made me unique
But the loss was not felt
Losing myself a bit each
Passing day
My image blurred
Along with my smile
I never missed it
You faded from my life
I never felt it
I existed without color
I had no dimension
My passion died
Exhaling its last breath
Spitting a seed
Into my barren heart
That grew into words
Not lost
Just forgotten
Waiting upon my return

Gypsy Mercer

JESSICA MILLER
I AM A POET

Some days
I am a poet
A twister of words
An artist of pain
Burning worlds filled with angry red flames
A hot July summer in a burning desert
Screaming for ice water... anything to relieve
These memories that insist
On still burning me in my nightmares
Other days
I am a poet
A creator of words
An artist of love
Burning worlds filled with sweet tales of dragons, ball gowns,
And a prince that would save the princess
From the nightmares of her mind
And her dreamy castles in the sky
Smooth and sweet like the taste of
Sweet iced tea in the middle of
A hot July summer day
Most days
I am a poet
Who set fire to the boxes and molds
They shoved me in and ended up saving myself.

Jessica Miller (Rediscovery of Wonder)

FOR YOU

This is for you
The ones who said I was worthless,
The ones who said I was just another hopeless statistic
The ones who told me I was and still am going to hell
When I left a toxic church environment...
Those who saw my pain, smirked and said I would never make it...
The ones who weren't there for me in my darkest moments
Yet still, have so much to say when they know so little
The ones who, when asked, say "I knew here back when",
The doubters... the whisperers... the talkers...
The pointed glances and disapproving eyes...
The gossipers... the naysayers...
The negative ones who still have my name dripping off the tips of
their tongues...
This is for you
Because
If you hadn't done all those things
I would have never found the courage
To look you in the eye right before I walked away
And say "Watch me"
And darling, please don't forget...
When they ask you about me...
And what I'm doing with my life...
Make sure you tell them
I'm doing just fine.

Jessica Miller   (Rediscovery of Wonder)

WARRIOR

Beautiful girl,
Don't ever let them tell you
That you are too much, too passionate...
You hold the stars in your eyes,
And every hope the skies have ever contained
In the deepest places of your heart
Where you carry a love so deep, so vast,
That even you, could not contain it if you tried...
The universe noticed and branded you a warrior,
A voice for those who cannot stand up for themselves...
And this? Is the magic they hate...
The one where they wonder, in stunning revelations,
How they woke up one morning
Only to find you on the ledge... speaking your truth...
This is both your beauty and your hurt...
And this is where you begin to change the world.

Jessica Miller   (Rediscovery of Wonder)

MICHELLE SCHAPER

SHIELD OF HOPE

When nightfall comes
and your loved ones have gone to sleep
Anxiety wraps itself around you
while all is quiet but your heartbeat
Thoughts appear like little armies
approaching the battleground
Tiny soldiers lining up
each with new weapons found
One throws doubt your way
another shoots bullets of fear
Swords of thoughts
pierce through your mind causing yet another tear
But somewhere in the darkness
hides your biggest shield of hope
protecting your defenses
bringing you new ways to cope
So when your heartbeat softens
and dreaming finally comes your way
May hope hold you through the night
For you to face another day.

Michelle Schaper

THE HANDS OF TIME

When there's a fire we call the fire brigade,
a wreck where someone's hurt,
an ambulance is called
and criminal activity calls for the police.
But who do we call for the souls on fire,
wrecked minds
and crimes of the heart?
Where are the sirens and rescue crews
when you're drowning in your own tears,
while thoughts blaze through your mind
stealing every happy notion,
when all you can hear is the sound of your own heart
breaking?
There are no emergency teams
coming to fix damaged souls.
There is only hope.
Let it find you
and seep through the cracks.
Let time cup your heart in its hands
and caress your mind;
And let the lips of life
forever kiss your soul.

Michelle Schaper

ANGELS SIN TOO

*"I want to keep you like a secret
and love you like a sin."*

Vanity takes pride in materialism and likes to stroke your ego, she declines invitations which aren't ball gown or tuxedo. Perhaps conformity taught her conceit, attributed by society, but it's not too late to learn how to see our inner beauty.

Envy wishes he could have all of your possessions, he sometimes hides behind his sister Jealousy and each of her obsessions. If you look deep into his eyes you'll find tears of discontentment, he need only find a way to his own truth, be self-confident.

When Gluttony comes to stay, his behaviour's not so pleasant, he'll feed on your addictions and focus only on the present. He lacks manners and etiquette, does not consider consequence, and has never learned the meaning of the word abstinence. But it's not too late to send him packing, tell him to take a vacation, then spend some quality time with his cousin Moderation.

Greed comes from a family with the surname Selfishness, they are known as hoarders and for their unhappiness. The only friends associated are Ignorance and Power, they all seem to want to rule or own the biggest tower. I hope someday they'll meet with Kindness, be introduced to Humanity, maybe find some Wisdom and get to feel true Empathy.

Rise From Within

Lust can burn you with a touch, her flames leave fingerprints upon
your flesh, will have you crave Temptation with her every breath.
She's often seen holding hands with Desire,
but a ménage au toi with Goals or Dreams helps Lust find love for
life and tame her fire.

Sloth puts in no effort, therefore reaps no reward. He is lazy and
lacks achievements, him and work have known discord. Perhaps he's
not been shown how to live to his potential, he might need reminding
he is worthy, to find his best credential.

Wrath hangs out with Vengeance who often accompanies Violence,
they pay no regard to their extremities and how they can hurt
Innocence. Wrath and his brother Angry should try to remember;
sometimes anger is just trapped energy, find ways to cope with
emotions,
without losing their temper.

'And there she was, somewhere between
heaven and hell, trapped in her
circle-shaped heart, not telling where
the cracks might end or begin.
Not Knowing if she might be
the Poet or the Poetry, the Sinner or the Sin.'

Michelle Schaper

MADAME K POETESS

AS I STAND

In the arrival of birth.
I am Screaming.
Every scream from here on in, hushed.

Noise is a burden, SILENCE... Silence.
A voice goes unheard, another child goes, unseen.
Innocence, fading.
What is this, I am becoming.
But I stand.
Observing, the living of those paving my way
Inhaling violence, gasping for kindness...
Save me, love, from the suffocation of despair.

To become what I feel, inside.
Not the cruelty, felt at the hands, of life.
To come out the other side, alive.

I am not you, my guides, but I learn, from you, my guides.
From the child to the woman that stands, here, as I am, today.
I learn from you, my guides. To save myself from you, my guides.

As I stand, the hand of you holds mine, when I am lost. You are kind.
In a place, that is not...
I learn from you, my guides. Blessed be, my guides.
From the child to the woman that stands, here, as I am, today.

146

Rise From Within

You are as gone, as much as I once was lost,
but nothing is ever forgotten.
Remembrance, my guides. I learn from you, my guides.

From the child to the woman that stands, here, as I am, today.
I am that child, my guides. Your flesh and your blood.
But it does not much matter, that I bleed for your love.
I am sold out of love, to prove to you, my love.
Is my suffering not enough?
For you, my guides.

Your addiction fuels mine, my guides.
The pain is numb, my guides.
In its place, the void of darkness.
I am the rage mirroring your unjust anger.
I am the guilt of abandonment; the blame that falls heavy on a child.
My guides

The unwanted, lost child remains, in the dark, reaching for light.
To return to the love in which it came from; above…
"It is not your time, love. Find your way home. Your purpose is here,
love. Seek, and you will find, love"
I learn from you, my guides.
I leave this life behind, searching for myself,
in a foreign place, my guides.
To become what I feel, inside.
Not the cruelty, felt, at the hands, of life.

From the child to the woman, that stands here, today.
I am free, my guides.

Rise From Within

My purpose, your love, has not forsaken me.

As I break the shackles – I stand, as I am… free.
Do you see, my guides? The strength in my rise.
From the child to the woman, that stands here, today.

Madame K Poetess

MIRA HADLOW

I WILL STAND

When you speak my name,
with disgust or disdain,
and shame rolls off your tongue
as easily as the judgement
that paved the road
from there to this,
when sanctimonious rage
replaces the compassion
that was my birthright, k
now this:

I will stand,
as now, as ever.
I will stand,
with bruised wrists and knees.
I will stand
for every wayward daughter
robbed of her dignity
by notions of obedience
and silenced grief.

I will not apologize
when my words
pierce the silence,
or when they are

as unbecoming
as the blood on my lips,
or on my thighs.

I will not bow my head
or turn my gaze
when my voice
makes me unfit
to claim my rightful,
silent place
at a master's side.

I will lay claim
to what is mine,
and hers and hers again.

I will cry out,
clear and strong,
and I will pray
that in some distant echo,
another voice finds courage to rise.

In that silence,
my voice, now as ours:
we will be heard.

Mira Hadlow

MARCH FORTH

My father used to say that March fourth was the only day of the year that commanded action. "March forth. Make progress. Put one foot in front of the other and DO".

March 4th, I did.

March 4th, I ran from a man who beat me for years. March 4th, I ran from a man who probably would have killed me. I bundled my baby girl into a car, kissed her father goodbye, and told him that I would be back in 2 days. He didn't say "goodbye", or "drive safe".

"If you don't come back, will hunt you down like a dog and I will kill you".

I hid my baby girl at a friend's house in another city, only half expecting to see her again. I left instructions on how to contact my family in the event that he found me and made good on his promise.

I didn't mind dying but I wasn't about to let her watch me get murdered.

Slowly, we rebuilt. Slowly I started to believe that I might live to see her first birthday. To see her learn to walk. Slowly, the death threats started to diminish and I remembered how to breathe. Slowly, I began to remember how to laugh. How to dream. How to live. How to love.

20 years have passed since then. Every year on March 4th, I am grateful that I found the courage to put one foot in front of the other and take action.

March. Forth.

Mira Hadlow

AN OPEN LETTER TO THE MAN THAT BEAT ME

I've spent most of my adult life trying to be free. Free from fear, free from grief, free from you - or my memory of you, and us. I thought if I ran far enough, hated you enough, crusaded against domestic violence enough, I would find my freedom. I thought that if I wept enough, raged enough, or told my story enough, I could break the chains that have kept me so securely shackled to what we were.

I realized that I could never be free until I was willing to release you. I've kept you here. Bound to me. Mired in years of pain, unable to be anything else, anything more.

I need to set you free.

The truth is that I loved you so fiercely. I have never loved anyone as intensely as I loved you. Somewhere inside me is that young girl who still does. If I set down my rage, I can see you through her eyes.

Rise From Within

I remember.

I remember living and breathing for each other. I remember days on end, just being, existing, dreaming. I remember your laughter. I remember how you would touch my face like I was a work of art.

And then I remember the rage.

I never understood it. It wasn't you. I could see you inside whatever you became, but you couldn't hear me. I tried so desperately to save you, but you could never hear me.

I remember when you used to come back to me from that place. I would be bruised and broken and you would weep and tell me how sorry you were - and I believe you were sincere. You were devastated every time you begged for my forgiveness.

I was determined to save you.

At some point, I realized that I couldn't. The lines between the man I loved and the man I feared started to blur. I had to run. I had to convince myself that you were a monster and that I never loved you at all.

Years later, when my hearing started to deteriorate and the doctors were fingering head trauma and a skull fracture, I hated you. When my world finally went silent and I could no longer hear my children laughing, my rage became all-consuming. I only remembered the man I feared. The man I hated.

I refused to face my own anguish, so I gave it your name.

I can't live in that place anymore.

I need to be free. I need you to be free. Free to heal, free to grow, free to be more than what we have been bound to. I'm sorry that I was in too much pain to let you go before now. I wasn't strong enough to face my grief.

I release you. I don't know who you are today, but the man I knew, was gentle at his core. I release you from all we were, from all the rage and regret and pain I have chained you to.

I forgive you.

Mira Hadlow

S.A. QUINOX

GIVING IN

Inhale them deeply-
the days in which you overflow
with laughter and love.
Keep them close to your heart-
they will form the bridge
to better days in times when
all you have is a pocket of
fading memories and the urge
to give in to the storm-
do not forget that you walk
with a strength still unseen
to yourself- and that it often
takes a good rumbling before
the mountain is birthed
from the chaotic depths.

S.A. Quinox

NEVER TOO LATE

Don't allow anybody
to tell you that it is
too late for you to grow,
to learn, to play, or to love.
The soul is timeless-
and knows no end to its growth,
or its yearning to love.
My dear, why don't you
take this very second
to exhale your pain-
leave it between these pages-
and know that you are
carrying the strength of
all of your ancestors and
past lifetimes in these
gentle palms- giving up
has never been part
of your deal.

S.A. Quinox

WE WILL HEAL

Please, do not pretend
to be a child of the light.
We both know that
we were birthed inside
the most scandalous of places,
kept hidden beneath
the whispers of our mothers
and locked away between
the walls of clenched fists.
We may have been forged
from the dark between
unloved stars, both you and I-
but please believe me
when I tell you that
we are moving past our eclipse
and will soon meet
the rising of a new dawn.
And we will finally heal
the broken on our lips.

S.A. Quinox

SARA PUFAHL

BREAKDOWN THEN BREAKTHROUGH

I was very close to death when I was suddenly yanked back from the gates of hell. I was set along a path that would guide my steps for the rest of my life.

I had grown increasingly more suicidal over the years. Thoughts had turned to plans. Finally, I settled on a plan that seemed full proof.

I was convinced I would never be able to work to support myself, that I would never be successful, never be loved, and that my life was a failure. I was ready to call it game over.

Unbeknownst to me, the universe had other plans for me. Rock bottom became my launching point.

I was introduced to a support group called Adult Children of Alcoholics and Dysfunctional Families. Suddenly, there were people with stories similar to mine surrounding me and sharing their experience, strength, and hope. A flashlight was turned on. A path out of the darkness was revealed. All I had to do was step on the path.

I decided to give it a try. To invest in myself. To choose life.

In time, I became employed, moved out of my toxic living situation, bought a reliable car, made more friends, and even became a manager at work. I was responsible for leading a team that made the company over one million dollars per year. Before that, I had spent the previous fifteen years enduring long bouts of unemployment and underemployment, due to chronic low self-esteem.

I found a reason to live but it wasn't in my new job. The job was simply a tool for survival. I found a reason to once again embrace my life in the rooms where the 12 step meetings were held.

I found hope again. I found ways to forgive myself, understand myself, care for myself, and fight for my best life.

I will never consider suicide again because I no longer judge my life based on society's standards. I'm on a spiritual journey to overcome fears and insecurities and learn how to accept and give love. I transformed into a warrior who fights for myself every day now.

I fight battles others may never know about or understand- and I'm grateful for each and every one. I'm grateful for each day, each win, each loss, each lesson. Today I'm alive because rock bottom was simply the start of my second act, not my last act on earth before my funeral.

Embrace rock bottom and make sure you have one hell of a bounce back.

Sara Pufahl

SARAH HALL

RUINS

There's so much beauty to be found in abandoned places.

I see stories in those crumbling walls, sadness in those empty halls,
sorrow smeared down windows
and brokenness scattered in the dirt across the floor.

Neglected and unkept, condemned and derelict,
yet exquisitely intriguing and somewhat stunning in their disrepair.

Just like those abandoned places, there are also such people.
Weathered and weary, battered and worn, yet somehow still standing,
refusing to ever collapse or fall.

And maybe that's why I see myself captured in those abandoned
buildings,
crumbling, cracked, and peeling.

Yet still, stunning in my unkempt beauty,
making no apologies for my damage,
as I stand here in my ruins.

Sarah Hall

SWEET BRAVE GIRL

You, sweet brave girl,
with tear-stained eyes and a tired heart,
take me for a lengthy stroll
down your worn and dusty path.

Walk me down your lonely road
of triumphs and tragedies.
Point out to me your traumas
like singing birds up in the trees.

Guide me through your darkest days,
and speak candidly to me,
of moments that brought you to the ground,
bleeding on your knees.

Share with me your story.
Give your words to me.
And everything that fucking hurts,
just a little space to breathe.

Bellow your voice,
until it's echo fills the sky.
Bring your pain some refuge,
and just a little light.

Tell me your story, sweet brave girl.
One day it will save a life.

Sarah Hall

LANDMINES

I'm not wired like the rest of them.
Those pretty girls with wide smiles and starry eyes.
Those girls, the sweet ones, who walk through the world
like they landed on a rainbow when they fell from the sky.

Light and bouncy, cute and flirty, yeah maybe they fake it,
but if they do, I praise them, because I walk with a heavy chest
and don't smile on command.

At some point, I lost my bubble and spark. I don't even wish it back.
Now, I like myself hard.
Dark and edgy, rough and worn, because gooey is for marshmallows
and my sweetness turned sour many moons ago.

So, here's to the women like me--the land mines.
Wired up in a tangled mess, red connected to green,
and trauma caught up in-between

Want to find out what makes us tick?
Say a prayer and take a risk.
Calm and steady, don't let your hands shake.
Push our buttons, carefully, we may just detonate.

We are armoured, we are explosive and we are strong.
Want to know how to love us?
Be prepared to diffuse a bomb.

Sarah Hall

SPENSER SPELLMEYER

DEATH AND LOSS

I somehow can't come to hate you
I can't come to hate your very being
Even though you've taken so much from me
You were like a viper in the sand
Hidden, just waiting to strike
Injecting your venom into someone I held dear or
Even being a spell, hypnotizing to make others do your bidding
You're a mischievous, vile bastard
Yet I can't bring myself to hate you
Even after everything you have done to harm and wear me down
Somehow I can't fucking hate you
You elude me, you hurt ones I love
You've taken ones I loved yet I can't hate you
It's almost impossible, but just because I can't
Doesn't mean I forgive you for what you have done

Spenser Spellmeyer

PALE KNIGHT AND ETERNAL FLAME

I am the pale knight who wanders an unforeseen path
I've had my fire, my very soul snuffed out by many,
yet I'm still living
The taste of iron in my mouth and ringing of steel clashing steel
Igniting the cinders in my heart, reigniting from defeat
I live for both the success of defeating a foe
and being defeated by my foe
I've faced many black knights and white knights on my journey
They have slain me,
but I always come back with my flamberge ablaze
With the fire of my soul ready for combat

Spenser Spellmeyer

STEPHEN REMILLARD

START AGAIN

I still see my future in your face,
Remember every kiss and your taste.
Promises said and plans we had made,
These thoughts refuse to dutifully fade.

It is ok though I need these to remain,
I need to see through my personal change.
I need to trace these scars a few more times,
I need to embrace fully those deep lines.

I kept building myself on piles of ash,
False foundations haphazardly cast.
I need this motivation from our past,
To build a future I know will last.

The lessons from these faces I have loved,
Where my only mistake was misplaced trust.
This is where I scatter those ashes to the wind,
This is where I truly decide to rebuild again.

I can only do so much and it all seems so slow,
Yet every day I see how this foundation grows.
I don't know how long this will take,
Or even how grand a structure I will make.

Rise From Within

What I am sure of is this work will not stop,
And every demon I see will be hungrily fought.
When my work does come to its end,
No force alive could ever make me start this again.

Stephen Remillard

POISON

This poison still lives in my veins.
Bleeding out leaving visible stains.
It is a part of me that needs sorting through,
Needs cleansed...
That is what I am trying to do.
I don't live here anymore and am happy again.
Yet I won't deny my thoughts from surfacing.
I won't pretend they aren't there.
I won't lie to myself and not face my fear.
What has been found isn't hate or disdain.
What has been molded from living in pain.
I bleed it out because it is all real to me.
I write it down because then I can see.
I lived with all of this and felt every bit.
I have times where I need to face some shit.
I will never feel less, care less... be less
For the sake of false appearance.
I will own every emotion and thought.
I will not hide one single bit of what I've fought.
I see how it would be an easy thing to confuse,
When what you read appears so angrily infused.
Those are the thoughts that come and go,
The ones I need to release to grow.
But tell me then what is it that you do?
What about the thoughts poisoning you?

Stephen Remillard

TARA ŞANSLI

I TAKE MY POWER BACK

I think
I was an amnesiac
Until I took my power back
I forgot my own tenacity
Somehow

For every time you put me down
I think you'll find I'm different now
But you didn't change me, I did
Amid the stress, I still undid the damage you inflicted
Savage, you were twisted
Like a gifted sadist, you had me sobbing and addicted

Each weakness you knowingly created
Each guilt trip you lovingly shamed with
Every tool
Every weapon
Each put-down you used to break with
I used each one, brick by brick
To build my greatness

But I'll never thank you for your part
In failing to destroy my heart

For every insult, threat, attack

Rise From Within

I take my power back

For every time you forced control
Fit me to your rigid mould
For how you broke my self-esteem
Made me redeem myself for being me

For each time I kept my soul intact
I take my power back

Cos however hard you tried to tame me
My wildness never betrayed me
I always saved me

For every time that I fought back
I take my power back

For every time I got back up
Knees bruised, covered in dust
Back straight, knowing I must carry on
No matter what

I'm not grateful to you no, I'm proud of me
I take my power back

Tara Şansli

VALERIE LEYDEN-MORFFI

CHAPTER 13: MARY MAGDALENE

I open the small ornate box
and run my fingers over the smooth pearls.
An energy surges through me, like a jolt of electricity,
triggering visions of lifetimes past.
Chilled, I wrap my red sweater around me tighter.

One thing I've learned is that no matter the circumstance –
whether we wish to freeze a joyous moment forever, or can't bear the
thought of life continuing without someone we've lost –
time still goes on.

At an early age, I knew I was different,
always feeling things in a very big way,
stronger and deeper than most.
A "gift" that has often left me feeling alone and uncertain as to where
I belonged... incomplete;
and I longed for something, or someone, to make me feel whole.

Passion coursed through these veins like the Mississippi;
there was something inside me I could not name.
Like a burning flame, whatever it was, drew people to me like moths
–
awe-stricken by this ever-glowing light, happy to feel just a little of
its warmth –

170

and this heart of mine, bursting with love,
was all too happy to oblige.
I've only ever wanted to make people feel good about themselves;
to know their worth.

Every relationship was entered with my whole heart.
Not looking for perfection,
I fell for those with a damaged past, like mine.
As much as I was looking for someone to save me,
I wanted to be the One to save them –
praising their existence, anointing them with spikenard oil.
And in the end, it was the tears I cried – heartbroken at having failed,
at once again not being enough, and being alone –
that finally cleansed them.

They would move on – I would remain
The world I knew ceased – Time would go on

I wouldn't give my love to just anyone.
But when I did, I gave it all.
There were times I was robbed;
A nefarious creature here and there, drunk with lust and greed,
attempting to extinguish this fire within.
Disheartened in these moments I would withdraw, feeling repentant
and hopeless.
But my flame remained and with each day grew brighter until I could
once again feel its warmth, and remember who I was…

Maybe now a relic, but my very name in this life means strength, and
I feel it every time the wind catches my hair.

Rise From Within

After all these years, and lives,
lovers past and present,
ghosts and demons tagging each other in taking turns,
I've finally found my true love…

I take one last look at those pearls,
close the box,
let that last sip of whiskey roll over my tongue,
and join my son for the game of Sorry he has set up for us.

For he is the one constant,
the missing piece,
my center of gravity –
the love of my life –
And through him, my legacy will live on.

Valerie Leyden-Morffi
(Whiskey + Empathy)

CRUEL INTENTIONS

She sat on the jagged rocks,
absentmindedly combing the water as she thought back on the latest
altercation, little waves washing over her wrists.

His words so pointed and calculated.
Each one meant to belittle, ridicule, and minimize her every thought
or feeling.

Now that she was older,
she realized what an insecure and cowardly man he really was.
He did the things he did to make himself feel more powerful,
in control...
like more of a "man."

She could rationalize it all she wanted...
It still hurt like a Motherfucker.
All she ever wanted was his approval;
For him to tell her he loved her and was proud of her.

But too many years had gone by,
and she was no longer that dependent little girl.
She had found a strength within
that would safely carry her over any waves that came her way.

Valerie Leyden-Morffi
(Whiskey + Empathy)

WARRIOR

"Why do you write?" they ask her.

Without hesitation, she responded:
"I write to stay alive.

I feel everything so deeply, there are raging rivers coursing through caverns within me, far below the surface...

Every betrayal, lie told to me, unsolicited or undesired touch, every slap or act of physical aggression felt, each broken promise, every criticism of not being 'good enough,' all the grief felt from loss, all of it, rises up into the base of my throat -
Overwhelmed and unable to breathe, some days it takes all I have to keep from drowning.

Sure, I could find relief by cutting, allowing the emotions to seep out in a slow wave of crimson.

But instead of reaching for a razor blade, I pick up my pen.
Using the blood from the fresh wounds those shards of emotions create, I put pen to paper and allow them to spill out, receding the waters within, allowing me to once again breathe.

The very words you admire for their beauty and resonation, are my saving grace."

Valerie Leyden-Morffi
(Whiskey + Empathy)

ANGELA FOSNAUGH

LIKE THE SEA

Our souls, like the ocean, meet the sky. Where one ends the other begins. Our love was like a beautiful sunrise over the sea but as the sunset fades into the night sky we realize that we are just two hearts that were set on fire. Our souls aligned. So beautifully we came together, so tragically we fell apart. I gave you my all but as each fragment of my heart and soul were returned to me, broken like glass, I then knew that as the darkness set in and the sun disappeared, what looked so precious not so long ago now looked tattered and torn and in that moment I knew that nothing beautiful can last forever.

Angela Fosnaugh

FORBIDDEN LOVE

While headed for the light, he tiptoed through the shallow waters, always looking to the shore, sifting through the sand looking for any seashells he could find. She, dove deep into the depths because that was all she knew, soaking up her own sunshine. For a mere moment, their hearts connected but their eyes never would, he was too focused on every shell that washed up on the shore while she was too busy searching for that special one. The inevitability is that the ocean always meets the shore but once upon a time, this time, logic is defied, remaining in darkness, he could not see, the long-awaited surf appears but he's too blinded by the pebbles surrounding the sea.

Angela Fosnaugh

ASIATU LAWOYIN

SENSITIVE SOUL

I sat there with heaviness in the pit of my stomach, the pain bubble in my throat, as tears were streaming down my cheeks. It was a scene that would repeat every time I watched Charlotte's Web as if I was seeing it for the first time every time. The moment Wilbur discovered that Charlotte would die after laying her eggs. It was a wound that I would reopen repeatedly, and with all Disney movies in childhood. As an adult, I would have that same reaction to the one instant that would evoke empathy and sadness even if within an action movie. To say I was born with a bleeding heart is an understatement. I've always felt the emotions of others, compounded with intensity. My feelings were always zero or one hundred, very little in between. This hypersensitivity to others also included my inability to look people in their eyes, as I would experience much more than most. I was able to see and sense their pain intimately as if it were my own.

My hyper empathy at first seemed to be a limitation for much of my childhood and young adulthood. However, it was attending Spelman College as a Sociology major that I realized I could use my awareness and empathy to connect to others that were marginalized. As a senior, I founded a support group for survivors of sexual abuse, named S.O.S.A. The more that I used my voice to express and relieve the burden of my pain, I was able to identify those that related, allowing all of us to feel validated. What I and others perceived as a weakness was really a strength.

At thirty, I began to consciously use my sensitivity professionally via intuitive readings. That later progressed to life coaching, followed by social justice work, finally morphing into empowerment coaching. Most recently, eleven years later, I have discovered that I am autistic, which is the root of my emotional intensity. I now specialize in the neurodiverse, fighting the stigma, while supporting my fellow sensitive souls to healing, acceptance, and pride.

Asiatu Lawoyin

FIST FIGHT

"What would you do if I stole (punched) you in the face right now?" she asked me in front of a crowd of peers. I panicked internally but didn't want to show weakness. My heart was pounding, adrenaline rushing, palms sweaty, I thought I was about to get my ass beat because this would be my first fight. The girl that was asking the question was Arianna, one of the many bullies that I had encountered in my childhood. At the time, I was fourteen at a summer science program.

Feeling like an outsider, compounded with people lacking understanding of who I was, while perceiving me as stuck up because of my "resting bitch face," and limited social skills, resulted in multiple hardships. I also was a petite, Black, girl, who was raised in a predominately White, middle-class neighborhood with the Nigerian name Asiatu (Ah c ah 2). I sadly couldn't have been more of a target.

By contrast, Arianna was a young, poor, Black, girl who was forced to always fight for survival, sadly it's all that she knew. So picking on me was quite easy for her and she did relentlessly until it came to a head in this moment.

I paused for what seemed like an eternity, trying to think of a comeback that would de-escalate the situation. I tended to fold under peer pressure, and/or experience mutism, but that wasn't an option in this instance, the stakes were too high. It felt like years passed, but it was just a few seconds before I mustered the courage and responded, "I am not going to lie, I would probably be on the ground crying in pain." Laughter then erupted from everyone, including Ariana, and from that point on she left me alone. She wasn't the first nor last of my social struggles but she was my only almost fight.

Currently, at age forty-one, the root of my social difficulties was finally revealed; I am autistic. My medical diagnosis, which confirmed my self-diagnosis, explained so many of my childhood experiences including the one with Arianna. I now understand why I always felt like an outsider, bullied, called "weird" and felt disconnected. But my story doesn't end there, having a better understanding of who I am has been validating and allows me to connect to others with shared experiences. I use my voice to advocate for those that feel like they don't fit. I am an Empowerment Coach that now specializes in the neurodiverse. I feel complete in all that I am, and at the root of who I am is my autism, which is my superpower.

Asiatu Lawoyin

BRANDIE WHALEY

ALONE

I think I began hallucinating as a way to find you again.
In the dark, the heavy shadows would blend in such a way
that I could believe you hunkered nearby,
just waiting on me to discover you.
The stranger who before, had been unknown to me began to take on
your nuances...I began to imagine I recognized you in his eyes.
In these and a million other unacknowledged ways,
I made you live again

When I heard you whispering my name in a crowd,
(Brandie. Baby. Babyluv)

It told me I could make you live again by sheer desire alone.
I began to embrace desperation tinged insanity,
Sought comfort in my madness, believing that, in it,
my prayers were being answered.
I began to look for messages in the sand- tried to find meaning in
love poems written for someone else.
Tried to find the missing pieces of the jigsaw puzzle before me;
the one you and I had created the pieces to together.
The one you had left me here to solve now--Alone.

Brandie Whaley

FRAGILE HOPES

We move in fluid, unpredictable flow- coming so close one moment
we could share a breath... A frozen glimpse of eternity; a nanosecond
in which we are shown the infinite, before being pulled apart,
Back to where we started so the dance can begin again.

We are God's creatures; broken and flawed,
full of the sin we have been taught,
made up of self-doubt and limited by the skin we are in.
We are damaged,
The signs of self-inflicted body art
Are never-fading tales,
Evidence of the love letters we have penned to ourselves,
Silent scars and angry bruises
The physical verbiage we use
When there are no more pretty words....
when we open our mouths and our voices fail.

Our paths, as yet, are unchosen
Our footsteps timid, our footing uncertain
As we wait to see what life has in store for us next.
We are broken, and beautiful, equal parts fear and faith,
and full of fragile hopes.

Brandie Whaley

CLINT DAVIS

FIRE

Relationships got the best of me
The World had me beat
I gave up on life
I was done
Circumstances brought me back
The Universe helped out
I lived again
I tried
Then the mountain faded away
The Abyss called to me
I tried to die
I failed
Wandering around I stumbled through
My Will called to me
I began to rise
I stumbled again...
Then I found the answer inside
A fire rose up
I lit up
I live
I feel
I thrive
I win

Clint Davis

RISE UP

It's not about who's wrong as long as it feels right
It's not about the victory as long as you're still in the fight
It's like I'm holding all the aces but I know I'll never win
It's all about who's still with you no matter how long it's been
It's hard to shake the shame when they all know your name
And it's never about who's turn it is to blame
Rise up, rise up
It comes from within
Rise up, rise up
Find your own skin
Rise up, rise up
Dig down deep
Rise up, rise up
It's yours to keep
I can't give you what you need, so take what you will
Even if your battle is always going to be uphill
When it feels as though the fight has been lost
You can't sit back to see what all this has cost
Move ahead with fire so you can conquer your desire
And be the only one who will never tire
Rise up, rise up
It comes from within
Rise up, rise up
Find your own skin
Rise up, rise up
Dig down deep
Rise up, rise up

Rise From Within

It's yours to keep
When the struggle gets too much
Pull yourself through
The only one who can help with it is you
Rise up, rise up
It comes from within
Rise up, rise up
Find your own skin
Rise up, rise up
Dig down deep
Rise up, rise up
It's yours to keep

Clint Davis

EMERALD DEVINE

ENOUGH

Someone pointed out to me I get angry at things they wouldn't.

People are different.
We each handle things differently.
Tremendously different from a man's point of view to a woman's.
Men have luxuries I can't afford.
Definitely not when you come off as a:
strong
fierce
and independent woman.
It's almost as if the limp dicks and empty heads like to challenge you
at every opportunity.
Maybe that's just my luck.

It wasn't just that though.
I didn't grow up typical.
I swallowed so much till I couldn't.
I emerged to be more than I could ever imagine with a few thoughts
that still linger.

Never again.
Not on my watch.
Try it.
See what happens.
~ laughs ~

I became more because too many sought to make me nothing.
Rage pales to explain what I hold inside me.
Incandescent.
Say it with me, incandescent. Begin to understand.
I generally think I do well caging it.
Not letting it damage people around me or taint them too terribly. I'm
aware it leaks out.
I'm not perfect and my anger is quick to fire.
Who said the other day?
"Who lit the fuse on my tampon"?
All you motherfuckers.
Every single God damn disappointment.
Every person who sought to place a boot on my neck.
Damn if I will even let pass a second
or even a remote hint of mansplaining, condescending, control freak,
boot on my neck bullshit from any human.
Whatever your gender may be.
If you don't like how I come at you?
You better check how you come at me.
I'm really nothing but a mirror at this point.

I give what I get.
Am I too much? Maybe...maybe...

And just maybe you aren't enough.

Emerald Devine

BOOM

I've never really had any moments where I feel that...
"I want my mom"...
No, that doesn't happen for me.
I call her by her given name, if at all.
My close friends and loved ones call her "The Cunt".
I think because it makes me smile.
She is one.
I have had moments, rare ones, but they have come...
Where I think and very much feel...
"I want to go home".
I never really had that.
Home was more a myth I have trailed after all these years.
Tracing it from books to therapists and back again.
It eludes me. . .
In the quiet moments of reflection when I reach for the kinder
memories of my dad though I think. . .
Home.
Not the most ideal of images by any means but I have a handful and
they are mine.
He's been gone now just as long as I had him alive.
21 years.
It's the tendrils of wood smoke finding their way to my memory that
triggers his voice just out of reach.
His face is easier to capture.

But his voice oh...
I so miss that.
Such a BOOM...

But everything with him was.
And well...

Maybe that's why I'm such a Spartan kick...

I am my father's daughter.
I miss you.

Emerald Devine

EMMA GLEDHILL

COME SIT WITH ME

Come and sit with me.
Sit in silence, or confess what pains you.
Talk about your aspirations
or reveal to me the images that haunt your dreams.
It doesn't make a difference to me, what matters is that you will
forever retain a seat beside me,
have a shoulder to lean on and an ear to listen to your thoughts,
even when you cannot bear to hear them yourself.

Emma Gledhill

EDGE

There was a day, not long ago, l thought I saw the end.
I saw no hope, no life filled with love, and no shoulder of a friend.
At the edge I stood, looking out, with no fear of what would come.
Then the realisation hit,
that I was strong and just for now my heart was numb,
I know I am nothing special, no beauty to behold.
But even I deserved one day, to have my broken heart consoled.

Emma Gledhill

PHOENIX MODE

THE GIRL I WAS

As I look back at the girl I was, I feel such a rush of emotions.
The girl that I was didn't know how cruel this world could be.
She had no idea about betrayal
until her life was seconds away from destruction.
The girl that I was never thought to doubt anyone
and trust me she paid dearly for such foolishness.
She was an innocent, a bud crushed under the soles of this world.
So yes, when I look back at her I feel a rush of emotions.
I miss her wide-eyed innocence and yet,
breathe a sigh of relief at its demise.
The girl that I was caused me too much heartache
but all that pain and hard-earned wisdom
gave birth to the woman I am today
and for that, I will forever be grateful to the girl I was.

Phoenix Mode

COURAGE TO LET GO

Have you ever had your heart broken?
I have and the walls I've built up around me since then
have been impenetrable.
I believed a lonely existence was better than a painful one.
I believed control would prevent further heartbreak.
I fortified those walls and thought I had it all figured out...until him.
I always thought that when someone worthy came along
they'd knock down my walls, barge in and I'd just know.
But I wasn't prepared for a knock.
That knock caught me unaware and off-guard
and almost as if in a daze, I opened the door.
And somehow it felt normal as if I was meant to answer that knock.
I still don't know what and how it all happened but I let him in
more completely than I'd ever let someone in and
though my mind was terrified, my heart was at ease.
Have you ever experienced sometimes you couldn't explain?
Something that went against all your traits and characteristics
and still, you found yourself doing things and saying things
that were buried somewhere in the recesses of your mind?
I have and if this ever happens to you,
I hope you allow yourself to let go and let things flow,
I hope you discover yourself and another who thinks just like you do
and I hope you both have the courage to let down your walls
and reveal your truths in all their beauty and grace.
Above all, I hope you listen to your heart without letting your past
color your present.

Phoenix Mode

KCL_WORDS

BARE

i stand (alone) with the crowd
dripping in fear and need
like pearls around our neck
or coated in glitter to hide the rot

we do love to pretend shiny
things make us more
but the weight of it makes
me want to tear my skin down
to clean bones

to scrape away the gluttony
leaving me small
leaving me old but new
barefoot as i walk out of the
now deserted city

strip me bare

i can live without it all

kcl_words

BIRTH

i let the dark become home

i chose it

rejecting the heavens
crawling through the
mud to nest myself at
the base of old trees

i lay there for years
skin getting thicker
chest hollow and
breathing slowed

giving up

even weakened
i remember starting to
cry in earnest either
in confusion or simply
because it was the only
thing left inside me

calling out
as i closed my eyes
(though maybe it was only parched whispers)
to those i lost or loved
to dreams, i couldn't quite recall

Rise From Within

to the sun
even my own name

an explosion
swept through me
ears filling with heartbeat
and i woke warm lush
moss cradling my body
a thousand tiny white
blossoms across my skin
birthed from the last
seeds of hope my heart
had been keeping safe

and i am reminded to live

kcl_words

LISA PILGRIM

BE BRAVE

Be brave they tell a 16-year-old girl
as the steel gray coffin hovers over a black abyss.
The final resting place of the skin and bones that are left of the home
that housed the immoral soul of the man who was her Father.

Be brave they say as she stands on knees that refuse to lock,
and she crumbles.
The bright red clay from a freshly dug hole
smears on her new black skirt.
The stain to be carried home like a souvenir from an event that she
had a front-row seat to that fate forced her to attend.

Be brave she hears from inside her heart
over the screams from lungs that make no sound.
She recognizes the voice and makes a vow to withstand any pain that
this cruel world throws at her.
Knowing that she will be brave
for she forever carries his love inside her heart.

Lisa Pilgrim

NEVER AGAIN

Little monsters weren't just in her head,
The big Demon let them in her bed.
The safe place where she lay her head,
Became a place where she prayed for death.
Sleep is something no child should dread,
But sleep doesn't come when little monsters are allowed to creep into your bed.

Now a Mother with a Daughter, her clone.
Vowing her girl never knows what she has known.
She fiercely protects from a protector's throne.

A budding young woman who's nearly grown,
Confesses a secret, their safe place is blown.
Protecting from outsiders who might do harm,
Only to find the monster lives inside their home.

Her heart fell out as truth slashed her skin,
Only shreds of a chest on which her guilt to pin.
Witnessing her child's anguish where innocence had been,
Unfathomable regret not seeing a monster in kin.

Facing their future with arms locked and a will to be healed,
They vow to see justice be served so it never happens again.

Lisa Pilgrim

CHOOSE ME

Home alone again tonight, we're chasing demons from the day.
I choose you. I Always Choose You.
You quench my fears, my pain, my insecurities.
Your strength is intoxicating. You lift me from my mind.

As I begin to feel safe, enveloped by your glow, my inhibitions fade.
Knowing you'll be gone by morning's light I urgently sample your flavor.
I hold you to my lips and savor every drop of warmth that you offer.
It's killing me to hide this shameful secret. This affair is unmaintainable.

With tears rolling down my cheeks, and a will to survive,
I rejoice as your amber liquid disappears down the drain.
I have found the strength to choose me.

Lisa Pilgrim

MARGIE WATTS

ENCOUNTERS WITH EVIL

My mother was my first encounter with evil. Home is where my heart died. I remember the exact moment. The day at five years old, I realized my mother hated me. It wasn't because I had done anything. It was because of who I was. I was a product of her drinkie girl past in the Philippines. I was a constant reminder of promises not kept and unfulfilled dreams. I just was.

As I got older, my second encounter with evil, I keep those memories locked so deep, even my mind dares not to go there. The best description I can offer, the creepy Uncle(s) you're warned to stay away from. Those that want you to sit on their lap and do unspeakable things. Everyone knew about it but no-one talked about it.

Finally, at 16 years old I escape. I decided living on the streets would be better. What could be worse? I was already being beaten and sexually abused, so I went for it. Then I met a man who I thought loved me and I could learn to love back. I thought I had found my salvation. Soon I realized only the view had changed. I had run right into the arms of my greatest evil.

Physical and emotional abuse seemed to become a magnet that

followed me all my life. However, nobody can break the Soul of someone who has lived in the bowels of Hell. Even Lucifer shows respect for me.

I learned to survive, overcome, and create my own Heaven.

Margie Watts

MATT FREITAS

DISASTER IN PROGRESS

With each new day, I'm becoming less and less of a person we like to label as a "work-in-progress" I'm learning how to adore my flaws and embrace them with a smile. I've come to realize I have a lot of broken pieces, and that I'm more of a "disaster-in-progress" but that's okay; because after every disaster there's a rebuilding season... I'll rebuild; but this time with more purpose and more grace, this time I will put my pieces back together patiently and kindly, and I will treat this change with the respect it deserves. I know I'll have to accept that some pieces may not return; that they just don't line up anymore, but this too, is okay. You see, this puzzle of mine is ever-changing; it's constantly morphing and drifting into the unknown. The uncharted waters can be quite terrifying, but I know being lost makes it that much easier to be found. I also know that being broken doesn't mean I'm not whole. So I say, bring on the storms and bring on the destruction; A work-in-progress is a work-of-perfection.

Matt Freitas

FIGHTING ROUNDS

Look, I get it. You weren't supposed to be here, but it's not your time to throw in the towel; No no no, these are the fighting rounds. This is the time you keep your feet loose and duck and dodge life's punches. This is far from quitting time. This is where you stand your ground and return fire, this is where you find courage and heart to keep yourself in the fight... Trust me, this life will show you no mercy, and no one said it was gonna be easy; but anything that comes easy is not worth having. So wipe the blood off your cheeks and jump back in the fight. It's time you show this life how harsh a butterfly can sting...

Matt Freitas

M. DAVIDSON

RIBCAGE OF THE RENEGADE

—Anissa's Reverie—

Even though your memory holds me hostage...

I find serenity in your astral captivity...

Narratives burst forth from the centrifuge of every vessel that has
ever left shore in search of the fabled paradise whispered of in your
embrace...

The pinnacles of engineering forged by mankind are fallible—
machinery warps in the truth of inferiority when dueling against the
human spirit...

Inequities sail and run aground against the cliffs of her boundaries...

Demons barrel through the sky and burst to ash when they collide
against the collective cadence of her truths...

An army of doubts march and gradually fall to their knees when
they're graced with the serenade of fleeting whispers that are cast
from her lips...in the brief but cherished roar of summers cataclysm;
they sing of only my triumphs...
You're lullaby resounds and winds through the hollow breathing life
into my conviction....whisps of red, shades of orange, fractures of

yellow, and the crucible of blue converge into the inferno that blankets me in your reality....a promise of Eden left pending...

Your countenance wields my flame the same way your hips sway and pull my gaze in tandem...

You're harmonic and feral dance forms an algorithm that underwrites your altar...

an altar made of me alone...

Erotic warfare is waged against my aptitudes, as the scribes of Eros and it's casualties bow their heads in reverence...

Poetry in motion....your spirits spellbinding sequence animates.... the sirens manifesto conjugates my comprehension....and gently cauterizes my own law...

the law that rules every savage, primal, and exposed facet and fiber of my shell...

A rugged dark visage...a mask for the facade of beauty...is rendered useless in the face of your true inspiration—the catalyst for merging your passions with mine...

As language leaves my lips, it splinters into diglossia....civilizations speak from a place I have no memory of living....senses are realigned with every succinct and forceful movement cast by you...

Even with every word at my disposal...with every picture I could paint with written doctrine...they are rendered defeated and are mere vapors in the face of your eyes...

Green...

divinity's archetype and a seat on the spectrum of color abandons whites perfection and golds false idolatry for the color belonging to life, rebirth, and the urge to thrive.....

The color green envelopes it's most vibrant and captivating luster from her gaze....foliage and cultivation are instructed to weave the fabric of what I've come to know as the cradle of intimacy...

Everything that's carnal....devoid of humanity....monstrous....and indicative of the beast within....the entity inside me, both ancient and primeval....once only painted with the stains of sins I committed to finding myself before you.... now is pierced by your intuition....quelled by your rebellion....invited by your cadence....surrendered to your magnetism ....and stripped of every striation of my blind obsidian muteness...

As she simultaneously embraced the personification of both a man's flaws and his allure....his veneer does not match the war within his core...

Green splinters widen and magnify into emerald sunbursts....her irises paralyze with wonder...

wielding gravity over truth and peace....until they fuse into a vulnerability only found in fables.....

Her eyes....erupting with the most defined silent thunder....articulate more than sound....or language....would ever conjure...

He could now ponder and peer into the myriad of ocular apertures that would lead him to a once devoutly elusive pathway out of the prison he forged to cage his nature...

He obliterates the apparitions which he's let bind him to harsh realities....to finally fall forth into the crescent of a woman's prayer...

composed....designed....inspired....and carved from her every desire...

Their obfuscated duality coagulates under filtered sunsets and Pontiac skies....their distinct alchemy of passion and archetypal heritage metastasize without boundaries....their emotions forge a new vein of truth....a story where horns bear testament to the pages in his book...not crown his image held by a world that shaped him....a story where her complexities and staggering power and hidden light would shatter the structures held up by failed promises....she could dance in freedom and chart a course for their bond....with nothing but extremities and polarized eye contact governing their chapter.....imagery constructed without sight....touch felt without contact....scents remembered without aromas....flavors defined without taste....and frequencies without sound color their space with merely the empire they forge around them...bound by the cataclysmic roar of resounding silence...

Wellsprings of excess and potential were instinctively indulged upon....wine ran to sweat....porcelain skin became a canvas for which her enigmatic biographies ran fresh and sparkling in subtle crimson tributaries....every bite that landed expanded the pupils of the other....galaxies once bound by the density of things made of the world...sparked....grasping ignition...bursting forth from unnamed lacunae and casting unwritten quotes upon their skin....freedom ran in continual, organic, and infinite movement....in the manner of endothermic exertion...

Her mane of flaxen marigold cascades against the scarred but devoted physique of her dark disciple....woven so distinctly by the winds that carried her wisdom buried deep within their waves. Electricity surged through her oscillating neurology commanding her legs to plant roots in cashmere blankets on either side of her newfound throne and anchor the animal within her dying to be released...

Passion lurks just out of sight...and salivates

he expanded his foundation and relinquished to her wish without any lapse in time or trepidation...diving further into her as he arched and surrendered control....surrendered his burdens....surrendered the most raw and intimate part of himself he thought he could give...but surrender it with reverence and explicit impact born of trust, awe, and absolute harmony.....
Afterimages saturate the air around them only to be thrashed ever so gently by radiating sensations that had never been named nor conjured in such a finite terramorphic expanse...

Rise From Within

Time yields its meaning to dimensions that no longer govern what is being created within the safety of four walls...

matte white Sheetrock and crown molding ache to be painted with the creation forged from this primal, artistic, and utterly beautiful exchange of

physicality....a physicality that now races through the minutes...enter hours...enter days...

on mere impulse and reaction...

Summer rays burst forth highlighting the heat of the season's tempest...animating the current of newfound love,

Virtues and conviction radiate and bleed like the ink being inscribed on the diaries kept in their youth with banal ferocity...much like her pronounced gasps found their melody in the alliteration of scattered raindrops pelting her bedroom window....they find their tempo in clock hands that detested permanence.....

A mural of swift nightfall...

The evil....the brutality....the depravity....and the desolation that had once perverted the strength of the renegade's spirit ...crumble and fall to ash in the immaculate and sanctified rapture of a woman's love...

It was yet to be known....yet to be written....that the beliefs and animus that was planted and cultivated in that room...would end up defining....shaping....magnifying......and forever altering life for both the Renegade and the Siren.

It was here on the path to Eden...that legacy would cast its will through time...bestow its blessing through passion....and purpose would synthesize ...fulminating unbound and barrel towards a new creed and permanent mortal bond...

It was here in their Oasis that their Creator intervened and spoke with such volume that sound was not heard....only hoped for in the silence and safety of their dreams...

"Child....Rose....New Beginning"....were the words that echoed through realities and enveloped the terrain of their contested paradise...

"To you, I grant the gift of Redemption....receive fatherhood and know joy. You were forgiven since before your choices were made"

"To you, I grant the gift of Healing....receive motherhood and know the meaning of home. You were destined to feel whole since before your pain was written"

Behind Blue Eyes rest quotes for the lost, depth for the broken, wellsprings for the baptized, and countless meanings yet to adorn the walls of the Heaven that Hell made...where creation grasps its new domain. Blue permeates the ocean where we emerged from, blue winds through our cultures and icons and illustrate the deepest of our emotions...and it paints the sky where we cast our exalted ambitions...

Blue is a color that keynotes the elixir of life...Blue carries the vastness of every unknown expanse in our world...Blue is felt in rising waves and is savored in torrential rains that cleanse what is best left to wash away. Blue crashes through the constructs and encroachment of mankind. Blue is stitched in the very fabric of life...Blue is what captivated her...Blue is where I found my power....my redemption....my purpose.

And above all...Blue made her feel things in ways she preached to be fiction...

Blue made her move in ways that she never new knew were possible...

Blue made her indulge in a manner that let her swim out deeper than ever and taste paradise...

no matter how destructive the inferno was that swept behind him...She was almost consumed by the force of what blue meant to her.....

It's said that Blue is the hottest and most destructive part of the flame.....

Blue became the personification of her life story....adorned in ornaments of tragedy. Blue fell from her eyes like rain. Blue claimed music that waits to be played...

the rhapsody of irony and afflicted duality of intent and force of will saturate blue in its truest shade of indigo...one that wears the crown of Sorrow...

cause hearing those songs that belong to him would invoke such emotion....an eclipse of such would simply be too much However, Blue now resembles hope.

Blue now finds its gravity in the fact that they illuminate the eyes of the most sacred and profound seed of creation that could've emerged from the collision of two lives bound together in fire...

In the ashes of the wake emerges the innocence of humanity...

It's the motive and coalescing zenith that now guides a man into fatherhood.

Blue is the catalyst....the cure....the absolute antithesis to every weakness and demon that once defined me...

Blue is my legacy and is cradled in the arms of the Siren...

Time is our canvas...

I am the instrument forged from the cabal of her wishes granted... A converted disciple of her sacrifices that made me whole and left hope burning bright...

Blue is our favorite color and the bond we share...and the color that illustrates the animus of love...

Blue shines from the eyes of our daughter...and the child we share is everything that the Siren, The Renegade, and the world are not...

Perfect.

M. Davidson

SURRENDER THE PHANTOM
—*Regrets Reverie*—

A wish is cast then laid to waste
Giving rise to lies that fulminate
His friends merge with the mists of time
While fear and fury forged his crimes
Phones provide a light into
some portals clear; some portals doomed
His gaze fervently scans to find a sign
Her eyes lost sight of hope in prime
In life, we try to write our scenes
Solidarity forever stains what's shared in their exsanguinated dream
He rests against his own demise
He prays in vain for a better time
He knew he faltered, he knows what's treasured
Now his devotion won't meet the needed measure
To break the cycle of afflicted eyes
He must move forward
One last time

Rise From Within

A cherub sits and smiles bright
Her mother watches, with a remnant of light,
Her oasis made, designed to last
When clashed against the sins of his shattered past
A binding truth showered the soil
A seed was planted within the coil
of burning chaos and the memory's passion;
As the ashes of Eden sing of her rapture...
As a father, he'll surely grow

Within this truth, he can cast away the fear of the unknown
So long as he retains a love refined
He'll walk forever to cross this great divide...
It's time to get up and make a difference.
No one is coming to save you from fear...
You either prove yourself and rise
Or prove your truth was the greatest lie...
For all his hope of what's in sight,
Despite what's lost he knows,
once again he WILL burn bright...

M. Davidson

ROMANTIC MERMAID

FROM MY ASHES I RISE

My heart has bled
times and times, and my soul has
drunk pain sip by sip
My heart has sighed
hidden pains and my soul has
cried over crisis.
My mind has handled
a crisis after the other
till the fall of me
To my doom, I may
submit for a minute or
two, a week or two
That may burn me out
but it is never the end
because I will stand
I will get up and
from my ashes, I will rise
Yes, I'll always rise.
In darkness, I won't
dwell for long; for a house of
light I'll keep looking.

Romantic Mermaid

BEAUTIFUL HEART

Beautiful Heart,
I know how pure you are!
I know how loving you are!
I know how tender you are!
I know how loyal you are!
I know much you have suffered over the years at the hands of liars,
cheaters, and pretenders.
I know that you take shelter from the world's madness in your house
of steel you built with bricks of lies and betrayals that were thrown at
you.
Beautiful Heart,
believe me, I know how many marks and scars you have bravely
carried after being dragged to unwanted battles and violent duels
thrown to the scariest pits of terror and the deepest sees of pain
imprisoned in the prison of others' poisonous thoughts
used by merciless narcissists and stupid manipulators
But the best part of all of that is the crown of survival you are
wearing.
Look how fascinating it is! It honors how fierce you have fought.
Winning or losing the fights is of slender importance. What matters is
that it honors YOU,
the heart of the survivor
the heart of the fighter
the heart of the true lover
Sincerely yours,
A Risen Heart

Romantic Mermaid

ROVEENA RAMSAMY

LIKE A PHOENIX, I RISE FROM WITHIN

I was maybe six or eight
He pulled me close and said
Shhh, don't tell anyone...
His lips touched mine
His skin felt mine
I couldn't comprehend
It didn't feel right
But he was my brother
So I kept it within...

I was maybe around 14
He climbed on top of me
And as I lay on my back I froze
While he fondled with my breasts
And his lips ravaged mine
His breath smelling of wine
Intoxicated, he could not remember
I was like his child
Thank heavens for his conscience
He got up and walked away
But the damage was done
So I told mum
She lashed out at me
Don't you dare lie
Make sure you don't speak

So I kept it inside
As the pain was too real

I was 16 and he was a crush
Let's go to my aunty's
We'll have tea and cake
Behind an abandoned house
He pushed himself on me
And asked don't you love me
And I froze again
He pulled my undies to the side
He tried to get in
I squeezed so hard
I prayed for it to stop
God saved me
And he couldn't get in
So he gave up and left me to be...
This time I learnt my lesson
I kept it in
But the shame engulfed me
And it made me ill

I was 19 and he spiked my drink
Am your friend you can trust me
So I trusted him
To take care of me
And take me to a safe space
This time the dice was cast
I tried to say no
He went on and I froze again

Rise From Within

And he took all of me
He then said it was wonderful
And confused, I convinced myself
That maybe I had led him
I thought it was easier to deny
What had happened to me
Little did I know ghosts haunt you forever
Until you bury the corpses

I told mum again
Cause the pain was killing me
Once again she lashed out
And told me I was a shame
To the family I was dead
Cause only bitches get raped
Don't you dare say a word
Else you will have to pay

I am now in my thirties
And it happened again
The man who swore to love and protect me
Has violated me again
I tried to seek support from family
And they pushed me away
You have to go to him
Don't you lie
You can't have the same thing repeated again

This time I decide enough is enough
I have hit rock bottom so many times

And even dug under the ground
This time I speak out
I won't let you stifle my voice
And I decide to take no more
Like a phoenix rising from her ashes
I now rise from within
And I shall burn anyone
Who's out to burn innocent souls

Roveena Ramsamy

STEPHANIE MARIE ADKINS

BURN

They say she is cold
Her heart a fortress
With no gold.
But her heart, it breathes fire and she has risen from her own ashes
more than you can fathom.
Her heart is not cold.
She just has yet to find someone who can stand close to her heat
without getting burned.
So, call her anything but cold.
phoenix, dragon, shapeshifter.
Female.
She burns away your expectations
And like Persephone
Flowers still grow beneath her feet.

Stephanie Marie Adkins

STEVIE FLOOD

YOU ARE GREATER THAN THIS

I just can't sit here and wait for you to decide your destiny.
I see you crumbling under so much wreckage- that it is killing you.
You want a life that nobody can ever dream of having,
And you escaping from the turf you so easily laid down for yourself.
Cry every night, Just to get there.
We break physically & mentally in this battle.
We shy away from society
because it's the only thing that is in our way.
Somehow we become insecure, about all our reveries,
No one understands!
But I will tell you one thing, You are better than this!
You know it, and you are going to get what you are praying so
desperately for.
You are going to be this amazing person.
No one might not know it yet, But deep inside you will rise from this
wreckage and become stronger than ever.
Plastic smiles will no longer be of use.
Because your achievements would have been your life successes.
Do not linger in the moment, because if you do;
You will not reach that greatness. Never.
Focus on your dreams, make them happen.
Today is your day,
To shine.

Stevie Flood

A CRUCIAL WAY TO DIE

Hey,
I've been meaning to talk to you for a while now,
But I haven't exactly found the right words to say.
Yes, I'm pissed off and hurt for a lot of reasons,
One in particular that I could never save my loved ones.
But the second reason is you.
I'm mad at you for not being the person you were before.
You chose your life because I was nothing to you.
I want you to know that I only want things between us to be calm;
But that doesn't mean by not taking the time to check up on me, and
telling me the way you feel.
I like hearing good news. The only thing I don't like is that I'm not a
part of that life.
You promised me a future.
I can't live in this kind of illusion anymore.
I'm only reaching out to you now because I have no other choice.
It's either to tell you that my deepest darkest secret is, that I'm mad,
well clinically diagnosed as mental,
Or it's to live in a life that I can't be with you.
It's been so hard over the last few months.
I can't sleep, because I know you're not here.
I can't keep my food down long enough; knowing that you are
happier without me.
Or it's the fact that I miss you so damn much it physically took over
my health.
Declining by the second.
Deteriorating into nothing.

I used to be this big beautiful woman who was so proud of who I was, & suddenly I'm just this broomstick with eyeballs limping in agony to get to you.

I'm lost, I'm confused, more than anything else. can't you see?

I don't upload pictures of myself in our chats anymore, because I am literally ashamed of who I have become.

I'm depressed by sitting here just waiting.

One excuse after another - I sat and waited.

I kept on saying you'll be back, the good news that you'll be back soon you say;

The bad news is, I'm afraid I won't be here much longer.

So if I don't answer your messages or your calls,

Don't be alarmed.

I'll be long gone, you won't know it until it hits the news.

That the sad lonely girl has finally taken her own life.

You don't follow the news, do you?

Then the only way to find out from the chatter of the crowd.

The moment that people start talking about it, you'll come to realize it was me.

Of course, when someone decides to take their own life, questions usually follow;

Social media will only be part of the questioning,

But then the loved ones that were left behind will have to answer.

That's you. Only you.

The first thing they will ask is, "Why did you leave?"

The second will be: "Did you know that it's possible for someone to kill themselves over heartbreak?"

Your theoretical answers would mean nothing to them.

Just that you are the one to finally realize that what you've done, will kill your life in an instant.

Rise From Within

You will be locked away, and there you will finally feel the tortured
pain that I felt for you.
The only difference is, You'll have four walls to keep you up at night.
Echoing back at you.
Echos that were in the back of your mind.
To drive you to insanity.
To understand that finally, that's what it was like for me.
You will curl up in a corner, rock yourself to sleep,
When day breaks, all you will remember is that lifeless body below
you is what drove me to suicide.
I'll see you on the other side.
Because there I can torment you, the same way you did to me.

Stevie Flood

JAY LONG

THE STORM

I am the storm
do not question my might
or the full force of rage
that has kept itself at bay
for all these years
dare those who choose to feel the wrath
do not question my purity
for it will cut you clean
and sever the ties that bind
each path traveled
has been chosen
forged by the fire inside
the miracle before you
is simply a soul finding its purpose
the cries you hear
are that of a warrior's heart finally weeping
left battle torn in the aftermath
of what some call heaven

Jay Long

THE ANSWER

As the warm fire lit the room around us,
I sat and stared into her endless eyes.
So many questions of lost love came to mind and I asked,
"How does one see the light, when their life is spent in darkness?
"When each rose touched has left a scar,
how can one love so freely?"
"When each waking moment,
is a nightmare, how can dreams come true?"
"And how can I be truly free,
when the walls I built have not crumbled to the ground?"
She held my hands in hers as if they were a precious treasure she'd
been searching for since her heart first learned to beat.
Her answer came with all the knowledge and wisdom of a lifetime.
She looked at me and said, "you simply believe."

THE JOURNEY

The mirror stares back with undeniable truth.
The years have forged a path
across each once smooth section of skin.
Memories and heartaches, granted wishes and lost moments,
all have found their way to the surface.
And although some roads were long,
each of the miles were worth living.
For we are not defined by the steps along the journey
until arriving at the final destination.

Jay Long

TABASSUM H

MY TENACITY

Let my tenacity be tested.
Let my patience be parched.
Let my esse be eradicated.
Let my living be lamented.

For I shall be salvaged,
By that very fragmenting -
fortitude that yet fostered -
somewhere inside me;

And not, overthrown,
by every one of those -
onerous ordeals that laid -
still to leave me slain,
and smothered.

For I'm the daughter
of that woman whose quest
for equity and zeal for justness
run in my veins.

I'm the daughter
of that man whose combative
spirits to sustain with sincerity
and persevere with probity

run in my veins.

I'm the daughter of clay,
and of callosity, crafted with
the competence of being fragile
and fortitudinous all at once.

Tabassum H

NEITHER

Neither do I belong to those fetters
of fragility furled around my feet,

nor do I belong to the shallowly
strength depicted by utter superficiality;

For I belong there, where each
tincture of my valor and vulnerability
knew to tread hand in hand.

I am a mortal moulding
and demoulding

to attain the best of myself,

and not the one

to corrode away whilst chasing
the calm or chaos of this world.

Who Am I but -
the daughter of clay,
and of callosity,

crafted with the competence -

of being fragile and
fortitudinous all at once.

And I shall not be the devotee
of the norms that have been
nurtured with sheer nonsense

but of those rebellions
that taught me to trounce
every worldly woe or wreckage.

Tabassum H

T H SMART

CLIMBING THE WALL

I ran away today, ran away from more than a man.
I ran away from shame. I ran away from pain.
I ran away from cruel words that cut at the heart and mind,
Words that would have me believe I am less than.
I ran away - from dreams shattered by yet another outburst.
I slipped out into the cold, dark night not wanting to be heard.
I ran to the wall, to the shut gate that seemed to confirm my fate.
Trapped, between fear and freedom – I could not go back!

In the darkness, I found a strength I never knew I had,
In the silence, I heard a voice I had forgotten.
It called me to look up, it called me to climb up,
And as I looked down from atop the wall, it asked me to jump...

Now you are at my window begging me not to leave.
Another empty apology spilling from your lips.
If I stay, will I ever have this moment again,
this choice to make again?

Time ran out on you today. As for me - it's not running away when I
am free.

T H Smart

SETTING SAIL

--a new journey beckons

I sat staring at my computer screen. No matter how hard I tried, I could not seem to focus on any task long enough to make any good progress. I was agitated - and tired, tired of the negativity, tired of the constant battle. Tired of feeling chained to a dream that demanded my blood, sweat, and tears but gave barely enough to pay all the bills in return. I had followed every get ahead tip I could think of: I had changed my lens, changed my seat, upped my game, contributed more, volunteered more, taken on more, cared more. I even tried caring less, which did not last long at all. Nothing seemed to satisfy the performance monster – it kept asking for more – all the while giving less.

Picking up my pen, I started to write. Thoughts cascaded out onto the page as I furiously penned all I was feeling. And then, as if a referee whistle had been blown, they stopped running around aimlessly, in what my father would best describe rather colorfully as ever-decreasing circles. They huddled together. From within this huddle, a single voice could be heard. It started out quietly, then grew more insistent. I knew it. I should have – I have heard it all my life. But this time there was a new boldness to its timbre, and I could no longer ignore its impassioned call to action.

Like a potter with a lump of clay, I quickly worked with my putty thoughts, moulding them with the digital tools in my arsenal to create a vessel that could set sail on a digital sea of content. I tested the waters. They were warm and welcoming – a good day to set sail. One action remained, and I carefully penned the only name that made sense. My own! I could no longer sit by idle, hoping, and expecting others to bear my voice off into the unknown. I had taken the first step; I had shown what I was made of.

As I scanned the horizon ahead, my sails caught a friendly breeze. I stood with arms outstretched, feeling the sun and wind on my skin. Others nearby paused for a moment, smiling as they caught sight of my thoughts, and with unmistakable joy, wishing me fair winds and encouraging me onward.

I stand at the helm, excited and inspired. A new journey, filled with my own dreams, beckons. The stars guide me as I set my sights beyond the horizon.

T H Smart

VICTORIA GIAMANCO-MOCERINO

ALONE

We've all heard the expression "when it comes down to it, we all come into this world alone and we all go out alone." I never bought it. As I saw it, we come into the world where most of us are greeted by parents who love us and have been longing for our arrival. Then, through the course of our lives, we meet others who are or become family, friends, lovers, husbands, and wives. And when death arrives, if we are fortunate someone, whether they are a loved one, a doctor, nurse, or caretaker, is there to hold our hand and witness our passage from this world into the next where I believe we are once again greeted with love.

But today was an awful day and I felt let down by those I love. But maybe today was a gift … maybe I stopped seeing the world through Pollyanna's eyes; maybe I grew up; maybe I became cynical, I'm still not quite sure. But today I understood and accepted the old adage about being alone as both wisdom and truth.

The truth I've discovered is that no matter how many loved ones and companions accompany us on our journey through life, no matter how many people we have in our lives who care for us, love us and whom we love and hold dear, none of the support and concern we often depend upon and take for granted is guaranteed to be there each and every time we need it. It is too much to ask.

The reality, as disappointing and frightening as it might be, is that when all is said and done we are, indeed, alone and we must learn to count only upon ourselves and our faith for solace and sustenance. This not only prevents us from being disappointed and unfairly angry or disappointed when those we love fail to "show up" every time we need them, but it also encourages us to develop a healthy selfishness. While we should always be grateful for the love and concern that is extended to us by others, we no longer need to depend upon that love and support to validate our decisions or raise us up when we are down. This "being alone" also forces us to actually ask for help if we are in need – not to expect it – and to accept caring and concern each and every time for the true gift it is.

The other facet of this truth is that we must take care of ourselves first before we can truly care for anyone else. It may sound selfish, but it is what is better known as survival. You will be happier for it and hopefully more giving because of it. Your self-worth will be grounded in how you take care of yourself and the value you place on caring for your own needs.

If you are always the first one to be there for everyone else, if you are the consummate "people pleaser," take heed. This approach to self-care is not as selfish as it seems ... it's really the same as when you are flying and you are instructed that, in case of an emergency, you should put the oxygen mask on yourself first before you place the mask on your child.

For a loving person, this seems counter-intuitive and very difficult to grasp. But if you sit back and really think about it ... think about it long and hard ... you will find the wisdom that lies there.

So, here I sit at the end of this awful day, where physical and emotional pain have taken their toll, disappointment cut through my heart and anger bubbled in my stomach only to discover that while the comfort of others is a blessing, it is I who must tend to the needs of this woman whose life I am living and to the soul that lives within me.

It is my birthright and my responsibility to care for this woman and cherish her as no other. This life is a gift and after all the years of telling her she wasn't good enough, or skinny enough, or pretty enough, or talented enough, or smart enough, I think I need to start being a bit kinder and making friends with myself because she's the one who's always going to show up and if I feel I can't count on her, I'm really screwed.

Victoria Giamanco-Mocerino

WAYNE THORRINGTON

CLEARING THE GROVE

I focus my will. Drawing in the mysteries of the ages, trying to get the world to tilt, yet still keep my consciousness from total abandonment of reality.

I miss that magic, the oasis of the intangible, the force our inner core longs for. I hate being this much in the world. My pen drips invisible ink.

There is so much freedom outside the box labeled normal.
How I long for the whisper of Gods or a breath that breaks the fabric of time.

Goosebumps rising on flesh at the touch of the full moon. My oasis, my escape, my manic perception.

Force-fed who we should be. Labeled unnecessary in the grand scheme of the universe, but we matter. Damn it, we matter!

We are not bequeathed or betrothed to the people or situations life has saddled us within our past. Just as simply as tomorrow has no reflection of yesterday. We may travel to the same destination, but each interaction is unique to its own rule.

Rise From Within

Fear lies, and Faith is our only lighthouse when fog-drenched shadows stretch across our picketed path. We must brush past the thundering herd of evermore.

I say again, fear is a liar. A briar patch of grasping thorns whose only purpose is to twist and ensnare our peace.

So take heart and take heed, grace lies along the edge of the overgrown. Trample down the underbrush. Make your own clearing. Sow your seeds of kindness, love, and forgiveness. Your flowers will blossom, and your shade tree will grow.

Wayne Thorrington

AFTER WORK MOMENTS

I know about the brambles and thorns.
I've crawled through the moors,
Scratched, bleeding, and filthy.
I've been in the muck and mire.
Blue eyes shining in the dark places.
Show me your soul.
Touch the headlong fires of past's pyres.
Let me stroke your cheek and kiss you gentle.
Silence humming as the world fades away,
Breath caught in its own galaxy.
Hold the demons at bay.
Wrapping the sky around your soft places,
Blanketing your scars with strong arms and
Soft brushes of madness understood.
Feel my gifts through my fingertips.
Compassion, mercy, and peace
Deliciously placed in extravagant care.
Unburden yourself for a momentary response.
I've been there, where you are.
Though not completely, I've seen the other side.
Hope dances freely on moon paths.
Silence drips honey as truth speaks in tongues.
I wish I could show you, lead you to stillness.
Keep you in my sweet embrace.
Let quiet quench your troubles,
As I kiss away the thorns.

Wayne Thorrington

LYNNE MEILE-VERSACI

SHOW UP

It's amazing what can be done just by being present for yourself. There may be days of struggle when things just don't feel as if they can get better. But remember to always show up for yourself. When you find your strength there isn't anything you can't do and you will find it allows you to be there for others on days they need it. Show up.

If a friend is hurting, show up.
When your kids need you, show up.
When a partner is feeling distant, show up.
When your community is in need, show up.

When your friends are hurting and you're not sure what to say, maybe all they want you to do is be there for them and say nothing-- just show up.

When your kids are acting out or seem distant, or confused, maybe all they really want is to spend time with you--just show up.

When your partner seems insecure, distant, or pushes you away, maybe it's for a reason--just show up.

When your community is failing or others in it are in need--just show up.

You see, it's not about what you can buy or what you can give, or bring to the table. Sometimes it's just about being there, sharing your time, which is our most valuable asset. Maybe it's about holding someone and telling them you aren't leaving. Talking to your kids and see what's going on in their life. Seeing how you can help move your community forward by volunteering. You'll be amazed at what can be accomplished with a little effort. You can move mountains by just simply SHOWING UP!

Lynne Meile-Versaci

ABOUT THE AUTHORS

C.N. GREER

Growing up in the Pacific Northwest, C.N. Greer has never been lacking in inspiration. In the last twenty years, she has taken that inspiration and expressed it for the world through the written word. An avid book reader, C.N. Greer is a fantasy writer and a poet. She hopes to share that love of fiction with her daughter. When she's not writing, she's spending time with her family and wrangling the fur babies that keep her life interesting. She believes in the human spirit and a person's capacity for strength and resilience, but she also knows those virtues can be hard won. She is an advocate for equality and compassion, and she hopes to bring some light into this world with her work of poetry and prose. Follow her on Facebook at facebook.com/cngreerpoetry/ and @cngreerpoetry on Instagram

ANNE BIRCKELBAW

Anne Birckelbaw, otherwise known by her pen-name A. Marie, is a former Journalist and Animal Rescuer from a small town in Michigan whose writing reflects her heart. She is a Victim Advocate who also donates her time to help homeless Veterans but claims her greatest accomplishment is her son, whose kind soul makes her endlessly proud. Anne's compassion is evident in her eye-opening writing about trauma and survival. Through a fierce spirit, her prose offers a voice, hope, and ink-spilled thoughts to provoke conversations needed by so many. Read more of her writing on Facebook at facebook.com/DarkInteriors and @ on Instagram @AWriterJunkie

COLEEN C KIMBRO

Coleen Kimbro resides in Dickson, TN in the United States with her family and a pack of Huskies and other eccentric animals. Coleen has been writing from early childhood and could always write a vivid story based on her surroundings to her beloved pets and family and friends. She enjoys writing short stories, poetry, and fiction, and is attempting to write her first book of poetry as well as a Novel. Coleen loves nature and believes in magick. She loves animals and genuinely believes in the goodness of most people. She longs for a place where there is no heartache or sadness and there is only freedom to be uniquely oneself. She dreams of living in a Beautiful Victorian Home with an enormous library filled with books where I could read and write all day long. Follow her on Facebook at facebook.com/Foresaken.Heart.and.Wandering.Soul and @coleen_c_kimbro on Twitter

DALENA DUCO

The path to addiction for Dalena was part trauma, part curiosity, part rebelliousness and her sheer fucking arrogance - "It will never happen to me" Needless to say, it happened to her. Decades on, her sons still don't realize they saved her life, from 800 miles away, they honestly saved her life. She feels it's an absolute privilege to be their Mum. Dalena's parents unwavering support always welcomed her home. The rest of her family and dearest friends, even though nobody knew if she'd make it out alive, they all always held out hope. Dalena's selection is her story and she us proud to say "I'm Dalena Duco and I am an addict." Follow her on Facebook at facebook.com/dalenamichelleduco

DONNA DAWKIN

Donna Dawkin has enjoyed torrid on-again, off-again trysts with the written word. Also known as The Poetessential Muse on Facebook and Instagram, she has found that exposing her inner desires, dreams and challenges across the interwebs has helped work out a much deeper acceptance and evolution of her true self. That hard, inner conversation is always the first one you should have. Only then will you truly know what you want and ultimately map the boundaries we all need, even though she jokes that she has none. Writing full time has always been a dream, and one day might even come true. Until then, a poem or two in this fabulous Anthology in the midst of all these incredible Poets and a published Chicken Soup for the Soul story, inspire her to keep those fingers nimble and to get back to writing from the deck of her liveaboard boat moored in the waters of Vancouver Island, BC Canada. Follow her on Facebook at facebook.com/thepoetessentialmuse and @thepoetessentialmuse on Instagram

CAROLINE CARTER

Caroline Carter has spent her life telling stories of survival, hope, and inspiration. A world traveler and avid reader, she finds herself most at peace curled up with a cup of tea and her dogs. With her husband's unending love and support, Caroline has found her voice and uses it to encourage others. Though writing is her passion, her greatest desire is to raise fierce, kind, and unapologetic children. To read more from Caroline and receive updates on new releases, on Facebook at facebook.com/CarolineCarter723 and @carolinecarterpoetry on Instagram

A. SHEA

A. Shea is an alias for Angie Waters, a writer/artist from Atlanta. Her work often reflects her own healing process as a trauma survivor as well as her fight to maintain mental health and live well with chronic illness. You can find her on Facebook at facebook.com/a.sheawriter, facebook.com/ashea.artistry, and @a.shea_writer and @a.shea_artist on Instagram

CHARLENE ANN BENOIT

Charlene Ann Benoit, a native of Newfoundland, Canada, began writing poetry at the age of ten. In 2004, she finished her first collection of poems, entitled, Pieces of My Soul. In 2005, she completed her first novel, When Walls Come Crashing Down. Since that time, she has compiled five other books of poetry: In Memory Of (2005), Shattered (2008), Between the Lines (2019), In the Hearts of Gods, Monsters, and Men (2020) and Blood, Tears and Coffee Rings (2020). She has also written a children's book, The Littlest Prince (2015), that is currently on hold for illustrations. She released a short fictional memoir called Death's Daughter in 2020. The Skeptic, her second completed novel, is expected to be released early in the new year. Follow her on Facebook at facebook.com/charleneannbenoit

DAWN P. HARRELL

Dawn P. Harrell works full time and writes for fun and also for healing and hope. She tends toward darker pieces, but that's only because she writes exactly what she feels. She has a soft spot for abuse victims and those who struggle with their worth, as these are parts of her as well. Dawn lives in Southwest Mississippi and loves being outside. In her spare time, she likes to hang out with her 2 grown sons and daughter-in-law, as well as her 3 rescue dogs. She enjoys working in the yard, devouring books, and all things horror. She is shamelessly nerdy, a longtime lover of the night, and you can find her at 3 am looking at the stars and contemplating her next piece or watching classic horror movies. Follow her on Facebook at facebook.com/seasonsofasewergirl and @sewergirl71 on Instagram

DIONA RODGERS

Diona is currently living in one of the most beautiful midwestern states of the US. Her home is filled with many children, including two fur babies. Diona has always had a love for writing. Her earliest story, Miss Kitty and The Cheesecake Fight, was such a hit with her partner in talking crime that he wrote the sequel to it! Later in high school, she wrote a thriller story that impressed and shocked her teacher. Diona's desire is that her writing will touch readers who have survived trauma, giving them hope and healing that she has found.

ELIZABETH

Howling Wolf Poetry is penned by elizabeth. The daughter of a self-proclaimed Grammar Queen and an artistic outdoorsman known for his watercolor paintings, elizabeth has been writing poetry for over 30 years – unbeknownst to most people in her life – until now. She has artists of different mediums on both sides of her family; some incredibly famous, and some just really good at what they do. With encouragement found in online writing and poetry groups, she began to reveal what only she had known – parts of herself and others in words of Life, Love, Loss, and Lust. Born and raised in California between the mountains and the ocean, she spends as much time caressing the earth as she does the keyboard. Her tolerance is high, her temper is low, and her love of animals and people is wider than any compass can measure. Follow her on Facebook at facebook.com/ howlingwolfpoetry and @hwlgwlf_poetry on Instagram

GROUND

Ground is an up and coming Canadian poet who is fervidly dedicated to her art. Since her debut, her style of rhythm and prose has captured the hearts of readers throughout the world. Ground acquired her passion for poetry at a young age from her late father, himself a poet, who encouraged her to express herself through writing. She is currently acquiring a degree in psychology and is an avid promoter of kindness and compassion. She hopes to captivate readers with her distinctive style and build connections through her work. Follow her on Facebook at facebook.com/poetground and @poetground on Instagram

IZZAH ALVI

Izzah is a full-time student of Psychology. She was born and raised in the beautiful and serene capital, Islamabad, of Pakistan. Living an ordinary life, the writer comes from a supportive and educated yet conservative background. Her ambitions and the city's dense trees and quiet mountains inspire her every day. Her writings have stood out at several writing contests in her city. She has been passionate about writing, especially poetry ever since her childhood and is always supported by her family. She started out with an enormous amount of self-doubt but was met with plenty of appreciation along the way which made her trust her potential. Recently, she has been focusing on body positivity following her own battle of body and self-image. She believes that this battle is never really over, we just have to emerge as an even stronger fighter every single day. We all have our own way of fighting, hers is through penning down the struggle whereby the chaos inside her flows along the ink.

JANDERSON

J Anderson has written poetry and short stories for as long as she can remember. Writing helps her process the tough stuff, and enables her to put into words those innermost feelings. Poetry captures the soul beautifully, and is such a subjective form of sharing. J enjoys knowing the words she writes can help someone else navigate through difficult times. J Anderson writes from the heart, and lays her soul bare and vulnerable upon the paper.

JENNIFER JENNINGS DAVES

A relative newcomer, Jennifer Daves is finding her place in the world of social media writers. However, she is not limiting her capabilities and is working to stretch her talents to the farthest reaches. Jennifer's writing is as often playful as it is brutal. Two sides of a completely complex and beautiful soul - one that invites you into the garden for tea but warns you of the dangers of sitting too close to the rose bushes, as she plucks the bloody thorns from her heart, one by one, and offers them to you. Whether it is prose, poetry or a song, she will definitely capture your attention as she serves up delicate pieces of her soul. Visit her website iworeabraforthis.com

KRISTIN KORY

Kristin is a Canadian writer who draws inspiration from both light and darkness. Her words are equal parts inspiring, empowering, and haunting. Her poetry and prose range from love and heartbreak, to healing, self-love, and growth. Kristin is inspired by nature, music and the unknown. She lives in Hamilton, Ontario. Visit her website kristinkory.com and follow her on Facebook at facebook.com/myhauntedskeletons

LINDI BAIRD

Lindi Baird is a keen genealogist who enjoy researching family trees and published her first book in 2007 with a second edition in 2014. The book was a tribute to an ancestor who was the First Landdrost of Beaufort West, South Africa in 1820 of which very little information was known at the time when her research began in the late 1990s. It was a gift to her deceased father who knew very little about his family history. In her spare time she paints in oils and do creative projects. Writing is a side hobby where she dots down her thoughts and emotions in a note book. Visit her website bairdsalindibaird.wixsite.com/website

EMILY JAMES

Emily James is the pseudonym used by Lori Weyandt. Lori's soul roams from the mountains of Pennsylvania to the mountains of North Carolina. She shares her life with her fiance Brian, her daughter Kirsten and her littlest love her granddaughter Miss Elliott Rose. Follow her on Facebook at facebook.com/akaemilyjames

ROBBIE J SHERRAH

Robbie hails from the Philippines and a poetic wordsmith that creates beautiful stories with his words. He is most proud of being a loving father and devoted husband. Always one to keep things in perspective, his writing brings you across several plains--each one heartfelt and open-minded. To read more of Robbie's work visit his Facebook page at facebook.com/RjSWriter/

RHAWN

"The trouble with Giants," says Rhawn, "is that there is no other place to find medicine." As a survivor of violence, she is a fierce advocate for healing the wounds of shame, blame, and voicelessness. As a woman, she has experienced life from both the edge and the centre—having worked in the straight-laced world of business and government, as a business owner, consultant, mentor, and now poet of the "gone and returning." Her writing carves paths through the solid rock of old tales in the mountains, etched by tears, finding a way down, when the only way out is down and out. Growing up, she travelled throughout Australia seeing some of the vast diversity of its lands and peoples. The mother of two wildings, she lives in Perth, Western Australia. Follow her on Facebook at facebook.com/strangechoes

NICOLE LABONTE

Nicole Labonte is a single mom to one daughter, and a 15 year old cat. She lives in a small city in Ontario Canada. She is a poet, but loves writing short stories and in August of 2020 she self published her first novel, the first of a trilogy, a modern-day fantasy fiction novel titled "The Wand." Nicole loves music; mostly of the post hardcore genre, enjoys playing piano and a lover of live (rock) music. Nicole is a dedicated mom, and a loyal aunt, sister and friend. She has many nieces and nephews that are loved as her own children, and friends who are loved as family. Nicole works full time in the cosmetic industry, and uses her off time to write as much as possible. She started writing at ten years old, and has only continued to find her passion through writing what is in her soul. Follow her on Facebook at facebook.com/nicolelabontewriter

SHARMANI T. ADDERLEY

Sharmani T. Adderley is an educator, entrepreneur, poet, novelist living in Nassau, Bahamas. 'Track Road Through A Pine Forest' is her very first publication of selected works of poetry, self published February 2020 via Amazon. What started out as a pastime has now become a passion as she currently has other works in progress. You can find her collective of poetry on Amazon.com.

SHAWNA OLIBAMOYO

Shawna has dabbled in writing from an early age but it wasn't until 2014 that her poetry really came to life. It was a very challenging year which included a partial amputation of her right leg. As the words poured out, they became her escape and her therapy. Shawna really enjoys writing poetry and being able to express herself with every heartfelt word whether it be of love, pain or inspiration.

Without the words, there is no light.
Without light, we cannot find our way.

VALERIE GOMEZ

Valerie Gomez considers herself an amateur writer who uses poetry as an outlet for emotional trauma left by the many abuses she experienced through her life. Her story began before she could remember, and includes molestation, physical and mental abuse and rape. She often refers to the people who abused her as monsters in her writing, and considers herself a warrior, not a survivor, because she's still fighting the demons of her past in her head. Valerie suffers from PTSD, Bipolar, Anxiety, and Depression which comes through in her writing. While she often calls herself worthless, she believes that she's strong even in her weakest moment. Valerie shares raw words honestly as a form of therapy. She also believes identifying is comforting, and key to helping others with similar issues simply feel human. She says writing is her only voice, and her screaming into a pillow is ranting online. Follow her on Facebook at facebook.com/justtakemetothetrees and @take_me_to_the.trees on Instagram

VERA E. VALENTINE

Vera E. Valentine was born in the historical and picturesque state of New Hampshire. The E stands for Erica, her given name. She began writing in her teenage angst years, after falling in love with the poet Emily Dickinson in fifth period English Literature class. After a cycle of toxic relationships, she began taking up her old poetry habit and started writing under the name Vera Valentine in 2014. Beyond poetry, she loves writing fantasy, supernatural horror and crime and mystery. She has a love for all things magical and can find the beauty in sadness, a super power of hers. She currently resides in the beautiful state of Colorado with her children, sister cats and defiant dog. Follow her on Facebook at facebook.com/veravalentinethepoet and @poetveravalentine on Instagram

S.L. HEATON

S L. Heaton is a warrior writer who has touched countless lives with her words of triumph and survival. She is a daughter, sister, mother, and proud caretaker of her precious fur-babies. As a daily fighter dealing with RA/Fibromyalgia and a survivor of domestic violence, S.L. Heaton's words give a voice to so many who feel they've been silenced. Her Facebook page and Instagram account have over 200K followers who have become like family to her. To read more of her words you can follow her on Facebook at facebook.com/agirlandherwords and @s.l._heaton on Instagram

J VERONICA CHRISTOPHERSON

Veronica is a Southern Gal, mother and grandmother born and bred in South Carolina..where she currently lives. An Army Brat who loves to travel, write poetry, photography, and animals. Particularly sugar gliders, her Clan consists of 7 thus far with a new arrival due in February. And according to her dear friend Mary, Veronica's full-time job is solely to keep Murphy and the rest in fishie sticks ;) as he in particular gets rather cheeky when not having any. Her dream is to travel, to write about and photograph everything that touches her soul

ZEN GAFSHA

Zen is a 41 year old wearing the girl scout badges of mother, wife and career woman whilst inhabiting sunny South African shores. She is a highly qualified risk manager, working in the largest seaport in the Southern Hemisphere. Zen's true passion lies in spilling words onto paper, she is the poet behind Layered Heart on Facebook and Instagram and the author of the book Addicted to Adam on Wattpad. Zen is a feisty, opinionated, witty, free spirited, liberal soul, an ambassador for sustainability, mental health and empowerment of women. She's fascinated with the out of ordinary and with human emotion, no matter how dark they may seem. Her ambitions are to explore the depths of imagination, of struggle, suffering, unrequited emotion and triumph and to trespass the boundaries of mind-sets by challenging regimented thinking and writing viscerally. Find out more about Zen's work at www.ZenGafsha.com and Facebook at facebook.com/layeredheart

ERI RHODES

Eri Rhodes is a wife and mother of two boys in addition to being a writer. With one foot in reality and one foot in the fairy realm, this pixieish poet turns the pain of her past and the love in her present life into rallying cries for warriors and reminders to victims that they have the strength and courage to change their future. She writes with the same passion and whimsy by which she lives her life. In her spare time, she enjoys reading poetry and nonfiction, crafting, and studying true crime. She also enjoys sharing her love for writing with her youngest son and her love for true crime and the paranormal with her oldest. She is a fierce advocate for survivors of domestic and child abuse and for those living with mental illness. Follow her on Facebook at facebook.com/pixiesecrets and @pixiesecretsmoonmusic on Instagram

FIJA CALLAGHAN

Fija Callaghan is an Irish-Canadian writer and artist who believes in embracing the magic of everyday moments. She lives between the seaside and the stars on a diet of dark chocolate and stories. Follow her at @fija.rose on Instagram

H.R. CURRIE

H. R Currie is a prose writer and advocate for self-awareness, healing, and empathy. She writes under the platform "Writing Behind The Looking Glass," that she uses as both a personal outlet and an offering of support and encouragement to anyone who may find comfort or recognition in her words. Her works, including Hope's Mirage, Lament and Quell of a Girl Unseen, and Little Swans, concentrate on perspective, personal experiences, and finding beauty in all that life has to offer, good or bad. Her works can be found at facebook.com/writingbehindthelookingglass and @Writingbehingthelooking_glass on Instagram

KELLI J GAVIN

Kelli J Gavin of Carver, Minnesota is a Writer, Editor, Blogger and Professional Organizer. Her work can be found with Clarendon House Publishing, Sweetycat Press, The Ugly Writers, Sweatpants & Coffee, Zombie Pirates Publishing, Setu, Cut 19, Passionate Chic, Otherwise Engaged, Flora Fiction, Love What Matters, Printed Words and Southwest Media among others. Kelli's first two books were released in 2019 ("I Regret Nothing- A Collection of Poetry and Prose" and "My Name is Zach- A Teenage Perspective on Autism"). She has also co-authored 18 anthology books. With two more books to be released in 2021, she is also working on a large collection of fiction short stories. Her blog can be found at kellijgavin.blogspot.com & @KelliJGavin on Twitter, Instagram and Facebook

L.E.

L.E. a truth teller. She speaks from the heart of her life experiences. She will not tell you what you want to hear, only what you need to hear, the truth. While kind, empathetic, and loving, she is not to be trifled with. Her thoughts are sharp like a sword and will leave you both genuinely entertained and pondering the depths. You won't be able to miss the meaning behind her words as she will pull you from the mist and take you inside the wonderings of her mind. Her perceptions are born of a range of experiences which have both crippled her and given her a soft experienced toughness and a huge coffee addicted heart. Her insight into the human condition touches every soul. She unashamedly breaks all the rules of writing and encourages others to do the same. She brings light to the darkness, wisdom to the ignorant, and love to everything she does. Follow her at facebook.com/madgirlsmusings and @ranting_wordsmith on Instagram

MANDY KOCSIS

Born and raised on the streets of Detroit, Mandy Kocsis currently bleeds poetry from She Hates It Here, Indiana. She's the only surviving parent of her amazing teenage son. She's seen more darkness than most, and it often shows in her work. Where most see darkness, Mandy sees the light within. She lives there. She writes there. And, someday, she hopes to find that love really does exist, but for now she's a non-believer. Legally deaf since birth, she's trying desperately to find a place she belongs in a world of face masks and silence. She currently has one book out, a poetic autobiography called "Soul Survivor" and is hard at work on her second. Follow her at facebook.com/mandyspoetry and @kocsismandy on Instagram

LYSSA DAMON

Lyssa Damon lives in Cape Town, South Africa, in the heart of the winelands with her family and assortment of weird and wonderful pets. Lyssa has written in some form or another since she can remember, starting with a poem about kittens losing mittens in a puddle. She writes poetry, short stories, flash fiction and has recently started work on a novel and hopes to recreate some of her stories as screenplays. Lyssa loves the ocean, talks to moon, and believes in magick. She loves animals and some people. Her ultimate dream would be to own a castle, with an enormous library where she can live, dream, and write full time. Follow her at facebook.com/linesbylyssa and @linesbylyssa on Instagram

GYPSY'S REVERIE

Gypsy's Reverie is a woman who considers herself to be a free spirit, wandering far off the beaten path and following her wild heart in relentless pursuit of passion and an authentic life. Her writing tells the tale of her struggle to climb out of the dark abyss and back into the light--finding her truth and herself again after years of feeling broken and lost. Always a lover of words and stories, she began writing to help herself heal and to chronicle her process of becoming. Gypsy's Reverie is so thankful to be able to share her journey on the road less traveled with other wandering souls through her words. It is her hope that her writing may serve to encourage, inspire, and/or amuse you while you travel through this life. Follow her at facebook.com/ascended.from.ashes and @gypsysreverie on Instagram

SHARIL MILLER

Sharil Miller is married with two beautiful daughters and three handsome grandsons. She loves photography as well as writing and tends to look at the world in a unique way capturing moments and memories not only through the lens, but through her pen as well. Sharil is adventurous and loves to travel. Three of her most favorite places for fun and adventures are Key West, The Outer Banks, and Myrtle Beach. She loves to go camping and has a cute retro camper to take time away to relax and refresh her soul.

THE RADIOACTIVANGL

As a teenager and young adult, writing was a passion of the radioactivangl. It was something that was given up for many years as well as music, but recently she's returned to with a vengeance. The two pieces found within these pages were written shortly before finalized divorce in 2018. A survivor of abuse of various types throughout her life, she's recently worked to truly take power back even more strongly than at the time of the divorce. She says healing is not an easy or quick process but it has been worth it and is thankful for all those who have helped during the process - they know who they are. Follow her at facebook.com/theradioactivangl

STEPHANIE BENNETT-HENRY

Stephanie Bennett-Henry is a born and raised Texas based writer who shares her personal experiences through writing and poetry. Stephanie's ink flows eloquently, creating beauty with her words of motivation and inspiration to raise women up, no matter what stage of life they're in. Stephanie enjoys spending time with her husband and her son, as well as their 2 dogs, 2 cats, and 2 goats. Stephanie is currently writing her first book which will be available in early 2021 Follow her at facebook.com/poetryofSL & facebook.com/ragingrhetoric and stephaniebennetthenry & @ragingrhetoric on Instagram

SUEANN SUMMERS GRIESSLER

SueAnn Summers Griessler is a US Navy Seabees Veteran residing in rural upstate New York. She is a widow, mother and grandmother (Tutu) who believes that no day should be taken for granted, and will forever be in awe of every sunrise and sunset she is blessed to witness. SueAnn is a published illustrator and accomplished artist whose original style of artwork includes varying mediums. She often melds her poetry and prose with her art. A quirky sense of humor mixed with a deeper sense of emotion helps fuel her desire to express her passion for a genuine zest of life, love, and hope. What started as the early steam-of-consciousness jottings and poetic lyrics of a young, hopeless romantic, her writing has evolved, often laced with introspection and multiple meanings. Follow her on Instagram @the_musing_palette

VAUGHN ROSTE

Vaughn Roste has written books, plays, poems, peer-reviewed articles, book reviews, program notes for CD liners and Carnegie Hall, and a doctoral dissertation, most of which never paid. His book, The Xenophobe's Guide to the Canadians, published by Oval Books in England (1st edition 2003 through the 8th edition, revised, 2016) just went out of print. Follow him on Twitter @Vaughn09187022

WIL R.P. MCCARTHY

Wil was born in Upstate NY. After his father reenlisted, he moved up and down the East Coast (USA). Never feeling like he belonged. He has suffered from Manic Depression since his brother's death when he was twelve and developed Schizophrenia in his early twenties. His writing is dark at times and will revolve around his problems. It started as a coping mechanism to deal with his issues and has evolved into a want to help others. He wants others to understand they are not alone. Visit his website thestoriesofaravingmadman.wordpress.com and follow him on Facebook at facebook.com/theravingsofamadman

AMY PASZTAS

Amy has self-published three books to date in the poetry/prose genre and is working on branching out and attempting a novel. She currently resides in Tennessee with her three and a half dogs (a yorkie only counts as half) where she recently moved to be closer to her parents. Amy's love for travel and nature photography, combined with her love of reading keep her imagination active. After all, sometimes we each have to create our own magic. Follow her on Facebook at facebook.com/PasztasA

APRIL SPELLMEYER

April Spellmeyer began to write when she lost her husband in 2011. When April penned her first piece of poetry the floodgates opened up about loss, grief, mental illness and trauma. While April expresses in raw, unfiltered emotional imagery she balances it with the beauty of hope, love, strength and healing. April finds several genres of music brings her words to life to tattoo them on the world. April is the mother to four children, three fur babies and Gigi to three grandsons. April enjoys reading, history, Star Wars and enjoying time with her family. April is the co-author of Soul Words - Eternal Soul Sisters Volume I, author of They Call Me Sister Kate, Sacrifice & Bloom, Scars of a Warrior. In 2021 she will be releasing Poetry Stained Lips You can find her books on Amazon and follow her on Facebook at facebook.com/eternalsoulsisters and @eternalsoulsisters on Instagram

DEBRA MAY SILVER

Debra May is a Poet whose works have been published in the Frances Anthology Australia. She has written her debut collection of poetry and black & white photography "My Rabid Fucking Soul" and is the founder of Ship Street Poetry. Debra has studied , screen writing , film production and marketing. A fan of Edgar Allen Poe, Oscar Wilde , Nick Cave, Neil Gaiman and Alice Cooper Her style is more often modern, raw and dark. She lives in Semaphore, South Australia with her Sausage Dog Colin. Visit her website debramaysilver.com and follow her on Facebook at facebook.com/debramayauthor

GYPSY MERCER

Gypsy Mercer has been writing poetry since college and has shared it via Facebook and Instagram for the last 5 years. She is the author of four books including 3 from the "Musings of a Gypsy Soul" series including "Into the Fire", "Surviving the Storm", and "Falling Rain". She has also published "The Lone Wolf", another poetry book that focuses on the wolf spirit inside us. Gypsy's prose takes a place in the genre that shows us that we can gain from life's experiences, whether good or bad. Our interpretation and internalization of the life lesson dictates how we will view them. She believes we can find positive and inspirational messages within, as well as warnings for future situations. We need to rely upon ourselves for strength, but share strength when we can with others in need. She finds love both empowering and memorable. She does not believe in staying victim to anything that lessens us as humans, and to truly "live" life as an active participant. Visit her website gypsymercer.com and follow her on Facebook at facebook.com/gypsysong and @mercergypsy on Instagram

MICHELLE SCHAPER

Michelle Schaper, from Western Australia, works as a support worker/carer for disabilities, (or as she says, 'enhancing people's abilities.') She is a mentor/advocate for mental health and domestic violence and has written poetry since her childhood. You'll find more of Michelle's work on Facebook at facebook.com/chellessoulpoems and @michellesoulkissing on Instagram. Her books 'Soul Kissing' and 'Fairytale Bones' can be found at some online bookstores.

JESSICA MILLER

Born and raised in Northern Michigan, Jessica Miller currently puts pen to paper in Colorado Springs, Colorado, where she works as a CNA and Massage Therapist. She was raised in a Conservative Mennonite Church, but left that setting when she was 21 to chase her dream of being in the healthcare field. Through poetry, she offers a closer look at betrayal, loss, heartache, compassion, love, hope, and survival. Somewhere between Northern Michigan and Colorado, she found herself gasping for oxygen, and the new life that the fresh mountain air breathed into her dying soul, is the same life that she uses to speak her truth today. Jessica's hope is that her voice and her story will be used as a beacon of hope, to spiritual, sexual, and domestic violence survivors everywhere. It is her wish that not only this, but all future generations of young girls and women will be as fierce in their determination and use their stories and voices to speak up for those who cannot speak for themselves. Follow her on Facebook at facebook.com/rediscoveryofwonder and @rediscoveryofwonder on Instagram

S.A. QUINOX

S.A. Quinox is a young Belgian and modern poet that writes for the aching, the yearning and the mad wanderers among us. She loves to write about the dark night of the soul, the parts that we so desperately try to keep hidden. Quinox can be found on social media through Facebook at facebook.com/saquinoxpoetry and @quinoxpoetry on Instagram.

MADAME K POETESS

Madame K Poetess was born & raised in New Zealand up until the age of 19, but has called Australia home for the past 16 years. Through the journey of life Madame K has found refuge & relief in the written word, a way of speaking without saying a word, a release of emotions that go unseen. 'Writing is to my soul, as breathing is to my lungs'. In 2019, 'Threads of hope - A collection of thoughts' was published, which was based around those that helped her get through the hardest times in life. Follow her on Facebook at facebook.com/madamekpoetess and @madame_k_poetess on Instagram

MIRA HADLOW

Mira Hadlow is an outspoken Canadian writer, self proclaimed romantic, and champion for the underdog. After an abusive relationship rendered her permanently deaf, she turned to writing as a path to healing and has become passionate about being a voice for the voiceless. Mira believes in ferocious vulnerability, unapologetic truth, and bravely facing ones shadow side. Mira is a quirky, creative soul and you can usually find her renovating a kitchen, losing her cup of coffee for the forty seventh time, or picking a fight with an authority figure. Her debut release, As Muses Burn is available now on Amazon. Follow her on Facebook at facebook.com/mirahadloww and @mirahadlow on Instagram

SARA PUFAHL

Sara Pufahl enjoys writing fiction and poetry in her spare time. She has been in recovery for depression, anxiety and avoidant personality disorder since 2014.

SARAH HALL

Sarah Hall is an indie writer and resides in Adelaide Australia. She has been writing poetry and prose for many years. She is responsible for Sarah's Collection of Scars on Facebook with over 20,000 followers. Sarah is currently judging and editing an anthology with Ship Street Poetry. Sarah writes powerful, empowering, emotive, raw and sometimes dark pieces. Her works are often inspired by her survival of domestic violence and other personal experiences in life, love and loss. Rise From Within is Sarah's first time being published. We certainly don't think it will be her last. Follow her on Facebook at facebook.com/sarahscollectionofscars

SPENSER SPELLMEYER

Spenser Spellmeyer is a young up and coming writer. Spenser penned his first poetry piece in 2019 to help him make sense of his grief from the loss of his father at a young age. Even though Spenser is young, his writing is mature, powerful and soul piercing. Spenser is a high school student who enjoys history, video games, music, reading Edgar Allan Poe and spending time with his family. Spenser has been published as a Spotlight Writer in the book Scars of a Warrior. You can follow Spenser on Facebook at facebook.com/spenserroyalspelly

STEPHEN REMILLARD

Stephen is taking the day's lessons as they come and doing his best to better himself every day. He is a father of two of life's greatest lessons and blessings. As a husband and father he is now on the Journey to find himself. In writing he finds a freedom to express himself completely, and then evaluates it and alters his perception and path as he goes. Follow him on Facebook at facebook.com/sharedthoughts69

TARA ŞANSLI

Tara is a wanderer of forests and lifelong lover of words; Tara cannot recall a time when she has not written poetry as a creative outlet. She has had several pieces published in books and journals and you can find more of her work on Facebook at facebook.com/ravenscallpoetry.

VALERIE LEYDEN-MORFFI

Valerie is a full-time working, single mother, raising her son in downstate New York, in the foothills of the Catskill Mountains. She is a passionate soul, with a zest for life, who loves and feels things in a big way, highly attuned and sensitive to her surroundings. Valerie developed an affinity for the written word at an early age. As an adolescent, writing became a catharsis. Restless, and a bit rebellious, Valerie finished high school early, graduating with her A.A. in Liberal Arts, at 18. In 2005, she earned her B.A. in Psychology, graduating Magna Cum Laude. Other passions include cooking, photography, traveling the world, being a mother, singing in the car, Irish coffee, and enjoying a good whiskey and cigar night! Valerie is a lover of the creative arts… all her writings are raw and real, coming from life experience and the depths of her soul. You can find more of Valerie's work on Facebook (facebook.com/whiskeyandempathy), Instagram (@whiskeyandempathy), and her Website (whiskeyandempathy.com), which is still a work in progress at this time. In December 2019, 13 of Valerie's poems were chosen to be published in the anthology, Broken Hearts – Healing Words, by A.B. Baird Publishing; one of which, "Light as a Feather," won the People's Choice award.

ANGELA FOSNAUGH

Angela is a creative and inspirational soul who discovered her love of writing at a very young age & her hope is that her words may inspire and touch the heart of each person that comes across them. She enjoys the simplicity of life and never misses the chance to take in a gorgeous sunrise and watch as it sets. Lover of everything that's beautiful. Follow her on Instagram @josiemarie120

ASIATU LAWOYIN

Asiatu (AH see AH two) Lawoyin is an autistic, intuitive, social justice warrior and empowerment coach that specializes in the neurodiverse community. Having been diagnosed with anxiety, depression and ADHD in childhood, she intimately knew the struggle to fit within the neurotypical world. Her life experiences shaped her desire to help those that feel isolated and oppressed. Her passions lead her to graduate from Spelman College with a bachelor's of Sociology. In 2009, she began to professionally coach clients to help them find validation, comfort, coping and healing. Later in 2018, she began to tackle systemic oppression from both sides while including ally education. In May of 2020 she self diagnosed as autistic and October it was medically confirmed. She feels her autism was the missing piece. She perceives it as her greatest strength that is at the root of both, who she is, and her work helping others. Visit her website asiatucoach.com and follow her on Facebook at facebook.com/asiatu

BRANDIE WHALEY

Brandie Whaley currently resides in Myrtle Beach South Carolina. She is 43 years old, and has written for pleasure since her teenage years. She has struggled her entire adult life with depression and addiction, and in November 2018 lost the love of her life to a heroin overdose. She honors him, as well as all the other fragile lives that have been lost in one of the poems published here. She is a lifelong fighter battling and for the most part, overcoming the demons that try to beat her on a daily basis. She is still fighting, she is still winning, she is still here, writing. Follow on Facebook at facebook.com/thewordsiliveby

CLINT DAVIS

Clint Davis is a former Paramedic who has seen tragedy and triumphs up close and personal. He can thrive in the dark but finds joy in the light. He lives for a laugh and dies when he cries. He believes in love but always drives it away. He loves humanity but hates people. He always adapts but never fits in. He wants world peace but would be fine with an apocalypse. Basically, he's complicated. More of Clint's writing can be found on Facebook at facebook.com/RoninDraygun/

EMERALD DEVINE

After growing up in a difficult world of secrets, pain and denials Emerald found her voice. She lives by the motto "There is always a way." and has learned countless times even when all seems lost; the story continues. Her message is to never give up, always seek a way forward and you will succeed. Emerald was born and raised in New York State, found home in North Carolina and adds, "I have one beautiful child who continues to inspire all aspects of my life." Visit her website oflostsouls.wordpress.com and follow her @dreameroflostsouls on Instagram

EMMA GLEDHILL

I feel as though a love of words, stories and books have been a part of me all my life. Books have always been a sanctuary. She tends to lean towards a more melancholy subject matter. She began to write as an adult, after the end of a marriage that she felt she had to escape from rather than end. Writing, mostly indirectly, about the experience and the person she has become since, became a cathartic exercise. Coupling that with finding the man that is the other half to her soul gave her a well of emotion and perspective Emma often draws upon. Being a happily married mother of two small children doesn't always allow her the time to write as she wishes but she wouldn't change that. However it is why it means so much to her to have been chosen to participate in this anthology. Follow her on Facebook at facebook.com/pentopaperc2g

PHOENIX MODE

For as long as she can remember, she's had these thoughts in her head and she always thought she should write them down but always put it off for one reason or another. During a particularly difficult time in her life, these thoughts could no longer be contained. They say heartache turns us all into poets and this hits very close to home for her. Phoenix Mode admits she didn't really know how to write but knew it was needed. It was no longer a want but a need. Looking back on her writing journey, it started off rocky but turned out well Today, she sees a growth in not only her style of writing but also within herself. She started writing under the pseudonym of Phoenix Mode because of a promise made to herself to rise from the ashes of all that had been and all that was and she hasn't looked back since. Follow her on Facebook at facebook.com/phoenixmodefromashesirise and @phoenixmode_poetry on Instagram

KCL_WORDS

Kim LaSusa, 49, lives in New York and is the mom of two humans, two cats and a dog that won't stop barking. She works in finance by day, and spends her free time in her garden, traveling and writing under the pen name kcl_words. A love of reading since childhood and writing since she was a teenager, Kim has only been sharing her work online since 2017. A poet with a penchant for the power of micro form, a need to capture emotion, writing has always been a form of therapy for Kim and she hopes to keep sharing her words with others. Follow her on Facebook at facebook.com/iamkclwords and @kcl_words on Instagram

LISA PILGRIM

Lisa Pilgrim is a self-described scribbler of sentences, a weaver of words, and a teller of tales. Lisa writes of love, lust, longing, loss, life, and throws in a pinch of laughter every now and again. A Southern Belle who has mapped the streets of hell, Lisa openly shares her victories and her losses through poetry and prose as she believes words are the conduit that connects us all.
Follow on Facebook at facebook.com/pricelesswords1

MARGIE WATTS

Margie grew up in the Eastern Coastal area part of Georgia known as the Golden Isles. She loved it there, living near the ocean. Even as a child she loved looking out past the horizon. It felt like looking at forever. Walking, sand between her toes and picking up seashells.

Just her and her shadow. "Me time", she called it. Butterflies was another of her favorites. Their beauty as they flew around. How they start out in the darkness of a cocoon and find their way out into the light as a beautiful butterfly. A reminder that darkness is not always a bad thing. There can be beauty from darkness. She was always an avid reader and a constant dreamer. Her debut book Wounded Butterfly was released in 2020-she never dreamed that all the tidbits on scraps of paper, notebooks filled with writings, would lead her to her dream of becoming an author. Follow her on Facebook at facebook.com/reflectionsofawoundedbutterfly

MATT FREITAS

Matt was thrusted into darkness. Unmotivated, depressed, and mentally unstable. Every day was a day that never seemed to end. He grew weary finding less comfort where he layed his head. He fell hard to his rock bottom where he was smothered for what felt like an eternity. Out of this darkness came one word that led to another; creating stories that had been eating at his mind. Torture has infinite opportunities to offer that he chosen to harness. He will prevail with his stories of heart break, and a painful past. Breaking up the static creating a pattern as the words fall in place instead of haunting him now. Taking what has caused him pain and turning it around. Chaos lives within him, but he has tamed his demons. Falling was the worst part, because he has learned that the bottom holds options.
Matt is an indie writer, poet, and wordsmith. You can read more of his writing on Facebook at facebook.com/restthewearysoul/

ROMANTIC MERMAID

'Romantic Mermaid' is a teacher by day and a poetess by night. She is a fighter, lover and believer of the magic of the kind heart and the power of a good cup of coffee. She likes reading, wriring, watching movies & eating chocolate. Follow her on Facebook at facebook.com/oceansofmyemotions & facebook.com/mywordsinproseandpoetry2 and @rihan_h_mustapha & @rm_coffee_and_poetry on Instagram

M. DAVIDSON

M. Davidson is a writer and poet. Born and raised in the Overland Park area of Kansas City provided the backdrop and setting for the life experiences that shaped, cultivated, and inspired the opportunity to find his creative animus. From an early point in his youth, he utilized language to overcome his speech impediment, wielding polysyllabic language to paint the concepts of love, loss, and awakening onto his canvass. Over time he would develop a style of writing that would become his own. His words are described as powerful, inspiring, and familiar to heart; able to capture the soul through pen and paper. He believes that cradling both agony and passion while casting their collective cadence in an exalted fashion allows others to view the extremes of life in an entirely new way, as a collective, not it's individual parts. Follow him on Facebook at facebook.com/incendiarycalligraphy

ROVEENA RAMSAMY

Roveena Ramsamy has experienced what she calls modern slavery for about a third of a century and has decided that life is meant for living and not be tortured in any kind of way. Having experienced decades of mental, emotional, physical and sexual abuse throughout her life from family, society and even organisations that were supposed to keep her safe, she now speaks up and refuses to live a life of abuse and pain. She promotes and fights for peace and a world where human rights are upheld and people are supported towards a life of dignity and positive opportunity. She is currently claiming asylum in the UK after years of what she calls torture and modern slavery. Follow her on Facebook at facebook.com/rovee.ramsamy

STEPHANIE MARIE ADKINS

Stephanie is the mama to 4 boys and wife to her high school sweetheart. Stephanie has always loved poetry and words. She finds inspiration in the real human experience and all of the emotions involved.

STEVIE FLOOD

Not so many people know Stevie Flood by her birth name, as it brings back horrific images of a past that she is so proud that she was able to walk away from. Therefore Stevie is the name that enables her to find the confidence and power to finally find acceptance. Stevie born in the UK, July 21st, 1986, raised on the northern Shetland island unst, & later moving to the southern state in the

Mediterranean, the Maltese islands brought her family together. Settled down, has a family. Something not too many people know about her is that she always put others before herself, as she believes they deserve to rewrite their own history. what was broken can be restored, and therefore her ambition to write became somewhat of a motivator. Stevie Flood started reading at a young age, shortly after finding out she's dyslexic, nothing pulled her away from her ability to write, as her father encouraged her to express herself through writing little thoughts out on post it notes. Years subsided fast, soon turning them into words of poetry. Today, having been found by some tremendous people she continues to write her heart out, by expressing her inner thoughts to paper. Motivating others with words of inspiration to the world. Read more of her writing at facebook.com/stevie.floodauthor

TABASSUM H

Tabassum Hasnat, a freelance writer of shortform fictitious genres. She sought far and wide in the search of something, that held her heart in passion, and thrilled her psyche ceaselessly. And that something was writing, and losing herself in those tedious tomes of law and literature. Soon, she was blessed to have the recognition of a published writer. She has completed her International Ordinary Levels in science under Pearson Edexcel, and is currently completing her Pearson Edexcel International Advanced Levels, along with law and legal studies. She has her own personal blog on the global platform of Storymirror Pvt Ltd. She has co authored in multiple international anthologies and book compilations, where her writeups have been published on platforms like Amazon, Kindle, Google books, Kobo, Barnes & Noble, and Notion Press. She is aiming to seek a wonderful opportunity to enhance & apply her writing skills in a dynamic workplace. Follow her on Facebook at facebook.com/tabassum.hasnat.10 and @_tashaa8055_ on Instagram

WAYNE THORRINGTON

Wayne was born and raised in Indiana, also spent time living in Missouri and now resides in rural North Carolina with his girlfriend and is a proud cat dad. Wayne has a great passion for the simple things: nature, wide-open spaces, and great story telling.

T H SMART

T H Smart is a writer, poet, visual storyteller, and all-round creative spirit. Both creative and strategic, she is as comfortable in the boardroom and training room, as she is in her home studio creating visual and written art. She weaves the threads of inspiration she collects in life and work through her writing. By sharing the beautiful messages that skewer her heart, she hopes to stir up others in love so they might be strengthened and inspired to run after the plans and purposes for their lives. She shares her suburban home in Cape Town, South Africa with her husband, daughter, and four furry friends. You can find more of her writing on her website Warrior for Worthiness (warriorforworthiness.co.za), Facebookfacebook.com/smartmuser), Instagram (tarynhaynessmart) or LinkedIn.

JAY LONG

Jay Long is a New York based author, poet, and natural storyteller. His creative voice can be heard throughout social media and online writing communities. Through his writing and work with other writers, he continues to establish himself as one of today's prolific voices. To learn more about Jay visit jaylongwrites.com or you can follow him on Facebook at facebook.com/writerjaylong and @writerjaylong on Instagram

VICTORIA MOCERINO

Victoria has always had a need for creative release. As a young girl she sang and played guitar in her church's folk group. She later participated in her high school's theatre program, performed in community theatre and sang at local events. Victoria always enjoyed writing. One day she stumbled upon a contest for a 'healthy living quote' held by the Maya Angelou Center for Health and Wellness. On a whim, she decided to enter. Much to her shock and delight, she won. Her words are on display in the Center's lobby alongside Ms. Angelou's books. With recognition from someone she so admired, Victoria toyed with the idea of sharing her writing more broadly. It is only recently that she created pages on Facebook and Instagram for this purpose. Her hope in sharing her words is to touch hearts and connect with others by letting them know they are never alone. Follow her on Facebook at facebook.com/victoriassecretmusings and @victoriassecretmusings on Instagram

LYNNE MIELE-VERSACI

Lynne Miele-Versaci is a lifelong New Yorker. Born with a serious heart condition, Lynne knows what it's like to fight daily. Her lifelong community work has gained her positions with the March of Dimes, American Cancer Society, and her local Senator's office. Her passions are music, writing, her two teen children, and her precious fur babies. Lynne's volunteer work throughout the Hudson Valley of New York has helped countless families and individuals. In 2012, Lynne was named the Go Red For Women spokesperson of the year by the American Heart Association. She is currently working on a book and is determined to bring hope to others both online and in-person (when she can) by sharing her story as a way to inspire and motivate.

ABOUT 300 SOUTH MEDIA GROUP

300 South's founder, Jay Long, saw a lack of one-on-one interaction for those seeking assistance when self-publishing their books. He noticed far too much misinformation being made readily available to would-be authors and companies trying to capitalize on the trust of inexperienced self-publishers.

300 South was begun with the hope to level the playing field for indie writers and authors. For far too long self-published authors were considered hacks – and that is because many self-published books didn't take on a professional look or feel. Whether that was from lack of knowledge and understanding or not truly identifying the full scope of what goes into a successful self-published project. Jay wanted to offer helpful solutions for indie authors stepping into the public spotlight.

The heart and soul of the company is its dedication to providing indie authors with information and services to help ensure their projects are top quality and ready for your readers.

The vision of 300 South is to guide and mentor determined writers towards the goal of being self-published. We assist you to find the best course of action to achieve your goals. Our services help ensure you put out quality, professional products to the world.

Visit 300 South Media Group online
Website-300smg.com
Facebook & Instagram-300SouthPublishing
Twitter-300SouthMedia

RISE FROM WITHIN

Made in the USA
Middletown, DE
19 December 2020